PROLOGUE

In the 1940s and 1950s, on any given day, a distinguished writer in search of tales could have called on Genevieve Chandler at Brookgreen, Elizabeth Navarro at Hobcaw Barony, T. N. Cox at Arcadia Plantation, and others who belonged to that small society of "people in the know"—individuals who shared life experiences with Low Country luminaries and held in their memories a wealth of old family history. This is not to say that over the years these individuals were never asked to talk about their memories, but when I called on them in the 1970s and 1980s, there was something in the eyes that said, "I'm glad you asked. I've been waiting to tell someone." These genteel overseers of coastal South Carolina tales were generous.

Many of the storytellers have since passed away, but in these pages you can join me on the front porches and in the drawing rooms. Through this collection of Low Country tales, I give you a glimpse behind the scenes of my research.

My husband Sid and I had great fun traveling the back roads. Each character we met was more colorful than the last—or maybe it was that we grew more excited the more we heard. During my interviews, I tried never to interrupt a story in progress, but there were times when I was unable to restrain myself and screamed, "Oh, weren't you scared half to death?" or "What did you do to get through this?" They kept right on talking, never allowing my interruption to break the cadence. The people I interviewed offered a spectrum of life in the distant and not-so-distant past—the rice planter aristocracy, people born into slavery, hurricanes of the 1890s, the renaissance that began when wealthy northerners bought up southern plantations to be used as hunting preserves . . . and so much more.

No one who knows me will ever believe my being at a loss for words. But when I reviewed my decades-old files—to find out if I had offered my faithful readers all the stories told me while traveling the back roads—the dust on the neglected folders silenced me. Pages stuck together from years of neglect. . . . But a yarnspinner doesn't walk away from transcripts like this!

I'm older now, and it is permissible for me to sit and think of those days when my husband Sid and I traveled the coast of South Carolina, interviewing long-time residents.

Low Country Voices

What Coastal Back Roads Folk Told Me of
Ghosts, Sea Captains, and Charleston Jazzmen

Nancy Rhyne

SANDLAPPER PUBLISHING CO., INC.
ORANGEBURG, SOUTH CAROLINA 29115

First Edition

· Published by Sandlapper Publishing Co., Inc.
         Orangeburg, South Carolina 29115

Manufactured in the United States of America

Library of Congress Cataloging-in-Publication Data

Rhyne, Nancy, 1926–
   Low country voices : what coastal back roads folk told me of ghosts, sea captains, and Charleston jazzmen / Nancy Rhyne.— 1st ed.
       p. cm.
   ISBN 0-87844-171-9 (alk. paper) — ISBN 0-87844-169-7 (pbk. : alk. paper)
   1. Folklore–South Carolina–Atlantic Coast. 2. Atlantic Coast (S.C.)–History. 3. Atlantic Coast (S.C.)–Social life and customs.
I.
Title.
GR110.S6 R43 2003
398.2'09757—dc22

                                                        2003016166

These friendly folks bared their souls to me. I remember them well. The same fire that burned in their hearts as they recounted a narrative burns now in mine.

In pulling my notes together I realized that bits and pieces of information from other research projects would aid the reader in understanding stories in this collection, so I added them.

Obviously, this is not a historical exercise. I am merely passing on legends. The Carolina Low Country is a magical place, and there could be no better setting for these haunting, sweet, and funny tales. Sit back, relax, and enjoy yourself. If a story or two urges you to head south for a visit, come on down. Once you stand by the murky Atlantic wiggling your toes in the sand, watch a pelican glide over the marsh and perch on a boat dock, and take refuge from the heat under the huge canopy of a moss-strewn live oak, you'll understand why I choose to call this place home.

Nancy Rhyne

Myrtle Beach, South Carolina

ACKNOWLEDGMENTS

My thanks to Lee Brockington, director of interpretation at Hobcaw Barony, who took time from her busy schedule to accompany us on tours of Hobcaw Barony and introduce us to people who had information we were seeking.

I cannot count the number of times I called Robin Salmon, Vice President and Curator of Sculpture at Brookgreen Gardens, to ask for her help. It would be impossible for me to express what she has meant to the Gardens and to me over these many years. Her commitment and unyielding standard of performance are a model for us all.

Genevieve Willcox Chandler graciously entertained me in her cozy waterfront home in Murrells Inlet on numerous occasions. And I spent days, sometimes weeks, at the Library of Congress in Washington, DC, and the Caroliniana Library in Columbia, South Carolina, poring over her WPA manuscripts. She was a consummate storyteller. Mrs. Chandler's brother, Clarke A. Willcox, Jr., was the perfect vessel for carrying the Alice Flagg story. I was blessed to have heard him tell the story many times. I am also grateful to the individuals who wrote me letters recounting their experiences at Alice's grave.

Always poised and elegant, Lucille Vanderbilt Pate is a true Vanderbilt. I fretted over how I would be received in her beautiful drawing room. She was down-to-earth and friendly and couldn't have been more gracious. George Young and the late Mr. and Mrs. T. N. Cox told me additional stories about Arcadia Plantation and the Vanderbilt family.

Mr. and Mrs. Edwin Fulton of Wachesaw Plantation became dear friends as well as benefactors. Not only were they a wellspring of area legends, they were great hosts. Olive Mancill of Georgetown, a busy school teacher, devoted an entire day to me at Hobcaw Barony, where she grew up. I'm forever grateful to her. Elizabeth Navarro, Bernard Baruch's former nurse, welcomed us into her home in Kingstree many times, and she always insisted that my husband Sid sit beside her on the sofa. She provided me with photographs as well as vivid memories of the Baruch family. Ella Severin, companion of Belle Baruch, spread a lovely tea in Belle Baruch's home at Bellefield. It would take an entire book to recount all of the Baruch stories she shared with me. The package of photos I later received from her was a real bonus. Lois Massey was especially close to the Baruch family. She told me stories so numerous they will never see print.

Others who are important to this book include Dr. McLeod Frampton, Mrs. Elliott, Rufus Thompson, the unnamed lady in the Charleston bookstore, Margaret Wilson, and Marion Whaley. Mr. Whaley's tales appear in many of my other books.

Sue Alston also contributed to my other published works—and this collection is no exception. Sid and I count among our fondest memories the hours we spent with Sue and her son, Will Alston. Without them, the Hampton Plantation story would not have been brought to life.

The late Sarah Finley Dowling went to the Jenkins Orphanage to work for "Parson" Jenkins in 1931. Her husband became president of the orphanage some time after Jenkins's death. It was she who told me the Jenkins Orphanage story. I couldn't have written it without her.

Nancy Jussely Lyle, of Rock Hill, came to one of my book signings and mentioned that her father had owned a large vessel, which transported passengers and cargo between Charleston and Savannah. She told me the story and provided copies of Captain Jussely's logs. My thanks to her for allowing me to share in her father's adventures.

Employees of Chapin Memorial Library in Myrtle Beach

have helped me day-in, day-out for more than thirty years. I especially thank Mary Owens and Lee Oates for their assistance in obtaining microfiche copies of old newspapers through interlibrary loan. Michael Coker, photo consultant at The South Carolina Historical Society, helped me obtain old photographs. Michael is a pro at his job in Charleston's Fireproof Building and as a practicing tour guide to the city.

There are others who are not singled out here, such as the people of Sandy Island, but their help is in no way less appreciated. Kudos to all.

My deepest gratitude goes to Amanda Gallman, president of Sandlapper Publishing, who has published many of my books. When I tried to woo Sandlapper with the proposal for this one, they paid attention. Barbara Stone's criticism and reliable editing have made many of my books readable. I shall always appreciate Sandlapper Publishing in the way one holds in esteem a comfortable and beloved home.

Finally, to my husband Sid—my life's partner and best friend—once again, I couldn't have done it without you!

When I remember bygone days
I think how evening follows morn;
So many I loved were not yet dead,
So many I love were not yet born.

Ogden Nash
"Many Long Years Ago"

TABLE OF CONTENTS

Mama Spoke in the Calmest of Voices   1

Letters from Alice Flagg's Grave   5

The Vanderbilt Who is Not a Yankee   17

Clarke A. Willcox's Favorite Alice Flagg Story   24

Only the Sculptures of God   29

A Most Prized Possession   35

The Misspelled Word   38

Walking in His Shoes   42

A Sandy Island Wedding   47

Roses Without Thorns   56

The Best of the Hunting Dogs   59

Baruch's Place   61

Deary-Deer   65

The Nurse Who Went Hunting   71

Little Hobcaw   76

The Origin of She Crab Soup   80

Healing George Washington's Horse   87

The Charleston Jazzmen   91

Where Are the People?   117

"Old Co'feedence"   132

Here Comes Captain Jussely and the *Hildegarde*   138

Author Nancy Rhyne with Will Alston.

Low Country Voices

Mama Spoke In The Calmest of Voices

"Not everybody," Miss Corrie would tell you, "made it through the storm."

Tiny, birdlike hands wrapped around the crochet needle and skein of yarn. Like a well-timed machine, the fingers pulled thread from the bottom of the skein and worked it over the needle in rhythm, as they crocheted the afghan. A fire burned on the grate. The little lady's words came suddenly, fast and sure, as though she had neatly boxed them in her mind and waited for years until someone asked her to tell her account of the storm of 1893. It was as if Miss Corrie Dusenbury forgot my presence in her Murrells Inlet home when she told her story.

Papa was a businessman and left that morning for Georgetown. Zack was here. Papa hired him to help Mama with the children. When Zack ran up to Mama and said the spiraling storm surge was coming into the yard, Mama spoke calmly and said, "Zack, place the flour barrel on the stove. Put the sugar box up high. Remove all lower dresser drawers and place them on the beds."

After Zack had done this, Mama said, "Zack please open all doors and windows." She turned to us and said, "Children, go to the stairs. Don't sit too high up nor too low down. Take the dog with you."

A fierce wind was blowing and the inlet had overrun the yard. The boiling Atlantic surge was churning like the open sea.

We children sat silent on the steps and watched the waves, like great domes of water, crash into the house through the open windows and doors. On the water were many things, including some chickens, Rhode Island Reds. All of this bobbed and swirled before our eyes. After a while, the water changed course and went back to the sea, sloshing by us. The chickens were still there.

Papa heard about the storm. Some-

one in Georgetown told him the storm
surge overwashed Murrells Inlet, knock-
ing down people's houses, and there were
few survivors.

Papa rode back to Murrells Inlet on
the riverboat *Mitchell*. He untied his horse,
which he had secured to a tree that morning, and started home. The going was
slow. Papa had to pick his way around
fallen trees.

Finally, Papa met a man who told him
we were safe. When he got home, we
were standing in the yard to greet him.
That was the happiest moment of Papa's
life.

I had listened to Miss Corrie's story in silence, but I was
unable to restrain myself any longer. "Miss Corrie, weren't
you scared half to death when Zack said the storm surge was
headed for your home?"

"No," she answered. "We children were not scared in the
least. That's because Mama spoke in the calmest of voices.
We were not afraid because Mama showed no fear."

I glanced toward a window and noticed that a light snow
had begun to fall. "Oh, Miss Corrie, we must leave at once.

We have a four-hour drive, and if it's snowing here in Murrells Inlet, the roads in Conway must be iced over."

Miss Corrie put aside her afghan and looked at me as though seeing me for the first time. "You can't leave now. You have to hear the story about Hurricane Hazel that crashed on this shore in 1954. I was evacuated by boat."

I promised to return and visit with this wonderful storyteller again. I was anxious to hear all she had to tell. But my schedule was busy and time went by, and when I finally made plans to contact her, she had passed away. I regret not hearing all her tales, but she gave me a graphic account of one of her best true stories.

Letters from
Alice Flagg's Grave

Clarke A. Willcox's telling of the Alice Flagg story was art
in its truest form. He sat in a rocker on the porch of his home,
the Hermitage—the house in which Alice Flagg lived and died—
and told the story to all who called on him. People came
from far and wide by car, tour bus, and boat.

My fascination with the distressed damsel took root when
I first visited Mr. Willcox on a cold January day. The amount
of research this man had done on Alice Flagg was stunning. I
returned to the Hermitage time after time to listen as he told
the story to others.

Imagine a cozy, white clapboard house with dormer windows and a front porch facing miles of marshland and the
ocean beyond. Picture oyster beds, ancient boat docks jutting
into the briny deep, and fishing boats departing and arriving
via Murrells Inlet. This was the Hermitage, the perfect place
to tell, or hear, the story of Alice—a place where the scenery
was as beautiful as the tale was haunting.

Willcox had written a book of his life at the Hermitage,

The Hermitage. Photograph by Sid Rhyne.

Musings of a Hermit, At Three Score and Ten (Walker, Evans &
Cogswell Co., Charleston, S. C., 1966). In the book, he cred-
ited his wife, Lillian Rose Willcox, with the section titled "The
Flagg Family of South Carolina (1784-1938)," but it was he
who sat on the Hermitage porch all those decades and told
the tale of Alice Flagg.

The first known Flaggs were from Norfolk County, England. In 1160 the name was De Flegg. Thomas Flegg, who
dropped the "De" from his name, came to America in 1637.
Thomas settled in Massachusetts, and his grandson, Gershom,
changed the spelling of the name to Flagg. John's son, Ebenezer

(grandson of Gershom), married a Newport, Rhode Island, girl and their son, Dr. Henry Collins Flagg, migrated to Murrells Inlet, South Carolina, where he married Rachel Moore Allston. Rachel and her first husband, William Allston, created Brookgreen Plantation, today known as Brookgreen Gardens. Dr. Eben Flagg, the youngest son of Henry and Rachel, married Margaret E. Belin. Of their seven children, four died in infancy. Two are buried in Belin Cemetery in Murrells Inlet, at the rear of Belin United Methodist Church. The three children who lived to maturity were Dr. Arthur Belin Flagg, Dr. Allard Belin Flagg, and Alice Belin Flagg.

Mr. Willcox used the adjective *demure* in describing Alice, who moved in 1849 with her brother, Dr. Allard Flagg, and her mother into their new home, the Hermitage. Alice's bedroom was upstairs. The dormer window provided an ocean breeze and a far-reaching view of the marsh and ocean.

Alice committed the unpardonable sin for a young woman of rice planter aristocracy—she fell in love with a lumberman, a laborer who owned no plantation at which Alice could become mistress. Although Dr. Allard Flagg forbade Alice seeing her young man, she slipped away for frequent rendezvous.

Dr. Flagg and his mother became suspicious of Alice's continued friendship with the lumberman. Dr. Flagg escorted Alice to Charleston where he enrolled her in boarding school. Not long after her move, Alice became ill and Dr. Flagg was

Photo by Sid Rhyne

summoned. Though she was frail, he succeeded in getting her back to the Hermitage. There, she died soon afterward.

While Alice's remains were being prepared for burial, a ring was discovered on a ribbon around her neck and given to her brother. Dr. Flagg, in a fit of rage, threw the ring into the murky creek that fed into the Atlantic.

According to Mr. Willcox, Alice was buried in her favorite long white dress in a temporary grave near the Hermitage. Her remains were moved sometime later to All Saints Episcopal Church Cemetery, near Pawleys Island. A flat marble slab, engraved ALICE—with no last name, no date of birth or date of death—was placed over the grave in the Flagg plot. According to the headstones, her brothers are buried nearby.

Many people say, because of the loss of her ring, Alice cannot rest in peace and revisits her grave in All Saints as a ghost. Some believe she was never buried at All Saints Church cemetery but was laid to rest at Belin United Methodist Church Cemetery or at Cedar Hill.

I have received many letters from people who say they have seen Alice, the ghost of the Hermitage. Some of the letters from Alice's grave follow. These have not been edited, nor have I corrected spelling.

> Dear Mrs. Rhyne;
> In June of 1990 I went to Myrtle Beach S.C. to visit my brother.
> While visiting my brother he took me to the grave of Alice Flag, I was quite surprised to find there was no grass around Alice's grave. My brother told me that people walk around Alice's grave at midnight during a full moon, in the hopes that Alice will appear.
> We were there in the afternoon of a very pleasant day.
> While standing at Alice's grave I felt

like someone was holding my hand, and putting a slight downward pressure on my wedding ring. This is the first time I have experienced anything like this. Many times I have gone to old graveyards to read the tombstones, but while at Alice's grave I felt a strong attachment to Alice.

I still think of Alice often, and if I get back to S.C. I will visit again. And I have a strong urge to leave flowers.

It wasn't until later that day when I told my brother of my experience, that he told me that ladies have experience a tugging sensation on their engagement rings.

Sinceraly
George
Riverdale, MD

Dear Nancy,
. . . My relatives are Flaggs.
Shirley and I visited Alice Flagg's grave late (5 PM) Sat Oct 28th. As we went in the cemetary to find the graves a shutter

on the church was banging & squeaking. Also a lone paper cup was blowing across the ground much as you see in scary movies.

Shirley said "You brought me to a cemetery right before Halloween." Later she discovered her earring missing. We said Alice took it. Shirley did not want to go back and look for it.

I am going to do some research on my family. It would be great to be related to Alice Flagg.

Sincerely,
Barbara
Downingtown, PA

Dear Ms. Rhyne,
. . . Last December, two of my friends and I had an unusual experience at All Saints Cemetery. Seven of us decided to head out to one of our close friend's family beach house one weekend right before Christmas of our senior year of high

school. After going out to dinner that Saturday night, I and two of my friends broke off from the group to make the several-miles' drive down the road to All Saints. After finally locating the church (it was poorly lit and quite empty around the area there), we pulled up and got out. I had no idea where the grave was since I had only been there one time before, a few years earlier and during the afternoon. Despite my poor directions, we noticed that there was only one working light in the entire cemetery, so we walked that way. Sure enough, one of us stepped right onto the slab before we even knew it, jumping back in surprise. Although I try not to take cliché things like cemeteries and ghosts too seriously, that place can be quite unnerving late at night. One of my friends wandered off a few feet away and the other began spinning mindlessly around the grave, poking fun at the supposed legend that if you spin around the grave of Alice a certain number of times, she'll tug on your ring. I recall looking over to my wandering friend and asking her something just as it happened: a gunshot went off, right there, in the cemetery. I've grown up around hunters and marksmen, so I am quite confident in my belief that whoever fired the shot was inside the cemetery with us. Although we never saw their face whoever fired the shot was inside the cemetery with us.

Caroline
Conway, SC

Dear Nancy,

Over the last few days I have been thinking about an incident that occurred to me many years ago as a college student. As I think about that event, I feel the need to write you during the daylight hours. You see, the event I am revealing to you involved Alice Flagg and my need to write during the day stems from the fact that the rocking chair directly behind me sat for many years at the Hermitage, Alice's home. What if that chair still held the memories of Alice? . . .

In March 1977, a group of friends and I converged on Garden City, South Carolina to spend our Spring Break. . . . As you can imagine, my friends indulged me and we made our way to Pawleys Island after dark.

. . .

As the instigator of this evening, I volunteered to walk around the grave and summon Alice while my friends stood there and watched expectantly.

. . .

As we were turning to leave, something got my attention at the far end of the cemetery. A faint light seemed to be floating in the lower limbs of a large live oak tree. My friends saw it also. . . . While watching the light, white lines seemed to flash inside our eyes. . . . We turned to leave, but I had to catch one last glimpse. What I saw terrified me; the light was no longer at the tree. It was now under a bush not 10 feet away and coming towards us.

Having totally lost my courage at that point, I yelled at my friends, "The light is coming after us! Come on, let's get out of here!" If the gate had not been open when we reached the cemetery's exit, we would have cleared it easily.

Cathy
Murrells Inlet, SC

Dear Nancy,

    . . .

I don't know if there is a family relationship or not but I hope someday soon to visit the area (Alice's grave) and maybe (if no one is looking, as I don't want to be hauled away by the men in white coats) talk with her a bit about the Flaggs.

Our side of the Flagg family came from Maine as far back as I can find. (The Alice Flagg in our family) was born 12 Feb. 1926 in Bradenton Florida. She spent 24 years in the US Army Nurse Corps, retired Lt. Col., and passed away 14 Janu-

ary, 2002 in Panama City, FL. She read
and enjoyed your books, and of course we
had discussions about possible connec-
tions both present and past! Who knows?

Birdie
Inverness, Florida

An old spiritual entitled "I Had a Letter from Heaven
Today" comes to mind when I think of Clarke A. Willcox. If
Mr. Willcox could post a letter from heaven, he might say he
saw Alice Flagg. She wore a long white dress, her hair floated
above her shoulders, and she was *demure*.

The Vanderbilt
Who is Not a Yankee

The road leading from US 17 to Arcadia Plantation house is unmarked and unpaved. The plantation is private except for the gardens, which are opened one day each year during the plantation tours sponsored by the women of Prince George Winyah Episcopal Church in Georgetown.

Those who are welcomed to the Arcadia mansion enter by way of a screened porch. From the porch, I stepped into the hall. Long floorboards extend the length of the hall, which is the center of the home. From there, one can look through the house and across formal, terraced gardens toward the Waccamaw River.

I came to Arcadia to interview Lucille Vanderbilt Pate, daughter of George Vanderbilt, granddaughter of Alfred Gwynne Vanderbilt, and great-granddaughter of Alice Claypoole Gwynne Vanderbilt (Mrs. Cornelius Vanderbilt who built the Breakers, a famous mansion in Newport, Rhode Island.)

A servant lead me to the drawing room, a massive space

at once imposing yet restrained, grand but unassuming. The
only sounds were voices of servants—happy, laughing voices—
coming from the kitchen. I sat tentatively, awaiting a prima
donna, someone who wouldn't dare break the code of silence,
who has long kept details of the lavish lifestyles of the very
rich under wraps. Within minutes, in walked a tanned young
woman in white shorts, shirt, and shoes. For an instant I
thought she was a daughter of the house. *Surely this was not the
grande dame.* Then it dawned on me, this young woman was
Lucille Vanderbilt Pate. She may have grown up wealthy and
coddled, but it didn't take her long to let me know she lived
by the same working-class wisdom as most Low Country residents.

Mrs. Pate gave me a tour of her home then brought out
the wedding photos of her daughter, Dawn. Not the type to
frequent Fifth Avenue in quest of fashion, to keep pace with
others in her social class, she admitted she took her children
to view Biltmore House and the Breakers, showplaces built by
her ancestors—but only as her family duty. Although she has
tremendous pride in the mansion in which she lives, she wants
it to be a home, not a museum. She saved the old family portraits for the last feature of the tour.

Alfred Gwynne Vanderbilt, Lucille Pate's grandfather,
loomed large in his top hat, driving a white coach pulled by
six horses. "He took passengers from London to Brighton,"

Pate explained. "The coach ran all summer, every week, although he didn't always drive." In another portrait, Pate's grandmother Margaret Emerson (Mrs. Alfred Gwynne Vanderbilt) is kissing her baby, George Vanderbilt, on the neck. The curly-headed boy is wearing an embroidered dress. Margaret is fashionably thin.

"This is my father when he was a little older," Pate said, indicating another portrait of her father George. "I think this yacht that was my father's"—pointing to a portrait of a ship with three sails—"is now in the Windjammer Cruises, prob-

Arcadia Plantation manor house is the original Prospect Hill Plantation mansion. Joseph Allston, born 1735, was the first to own this property. His son, Thomas, came into possession of the plantation and built the beautiful mansion that is owned by Lucille Vanderbilt Pate today. Photograph by Sid Rhyne.

ably named *The Yankee Clipper*. She may still be sailing."

The portraits, framed in heavy wood, are huge, some four or five feet high. After pointing out another of Margaret Emerson, with jet black wavy hair, as handsome as any portrait hanging on a private wall, Pate moved to the likeness of a man who seemed to sit in watch, with a benevolent eye.

Three of the carriages that belonged to Alfred Gwynne Vanderbilt are displayed in the Arcadia stableyard. Vanderbilt enjoyed his collection of carriages in this country and abroad. He was especially skillful at driving a four-in-hand, holding the reins on four horses as they pulled a carriage. The Vanderbilt collection of carriages is kept at Arcadia, and a huge portrait of him driving between London and Brighton, England, hangs on a dining room wall in the mansion. He wore a top hat, white coat, black britches, all very dressy. He took passengers from London to Brighton by six horses. His wife accompanied him on the first trip, and his granddaughter, Lucile Vanderbilt Pate, has a film of that ride. The very coach in the portrait is in her collection at Arcadia. Photograph by Sid Rhyne.

"This is the Commodore," she said. "Very determined. The nose is definitely correct. You always see him as an older man, heavier, but this seems to be him as a young man." The Commodore, Cornelius Vanderbilt, who became known as "the king of Long Island Sound" after he amassed a spectacular fleet of boats and started the Vanderbilt dynasty, seemed to approve of Pate and her interests.

Pate didn't always feel that southern people approved of her. She summed up her feelings on becoming a southerner. "Alice Claypoole Gwynne Vanderbilt, the mother of my grandfather Alfred, is the lady who gave me my place among the South Carolina aristocracy. When I came down here to Arcadia Plantation, some people said, 'Oh, you're a Yankee,' and I said, 'Oh, I can't be.' And then I found out about Rachel Moore Allston Flagg, who along with her husband created Brookgreen Plantation. Rachel was Alice Vanderbilt's great-grandmother. Was I glad to find Rachel!"

ADDENDUM:

When Pate mentioned that Rachel Moore Allston Flagg was her great-grandmother's great-grandmother, it occurred to me that Rachel was Alice Flagg's grandmother. I was excited to learn that Alice Flagg and Alice Vanderbilt had a common relative in the South Carolina Low Country. My husband Sid and I visited the Breakers in Newport, Rhode Is-

land. I informed the interpreter that I was from South Carolina and wanted to see anything they had on Rachel. He led
us to the Billiard Room, where a portrait of Rachel hung on
the wall. A collection of other Flagg family portraits hung
there as well. The portraits are believed to have previously
graced the walls of the manor house at Brookgreen Plantation and historic homes in Newport. By the 1950s they were
placed at The Breakers by Countess László Széchényi. The
book *The Flagg Family: An Artistic Legacy And The Provenance*

The Breakers, Newport, Rhode Island. Preservation Society of Newport County
photo by John Hopf.

Of A Collection, Introduction by Countess Anthony Szápáry, Essay and Catalogue by Dara L.D. Powell, August 1986, was for sale. Of course, I bought one. Back at home in Myrtle Beach I studied the family tree and discovered that the two Alices—Vanderbilt and Flagg—indeed had a common ancestor.

Still not quite satisfied, I wrote The Rhode Island Historical Society. My query was answered immediately.

> Dear Mrs. Rhyne:
> I have found that Mrs. Cornelius Vanderbilt was the great-great granddaughter of Ebenezer Flagg and Mary Ward Flagg, therefore making her the great-granddaughter of Dr. Henry Collins Flagg and Rachel Moore Allston Flagg.
>
> Marilyn I. Glantz
> Tech. Services Asst.

As I left Arcadia Plantation the day of my visit, I was thinking that Lucile Vanderbilt Pate exudes the warmth of a true Southerner, with or without Rachel Moore Alston Flagg.

Clarke A. Willcox's Favorite Alice Flagg Story

═══════════════════

On November 9, 1982, having visited the Hermitage many times, I called at the home of Clarke A. Willcox and asked if he would share with me his favorite tale of Alice Flagg.

Yes, it was about two years ago. They were lovely girls from Queens College in Charlotte, North Carolina. They came all the way back down here to the Hermitage and told me what happened at Alice's grave.

For years we have had teenagers by the hundreds come to our house. They go down to Alice's grave and communicate with her spirit. If they go down there and think of it as a joke, they don't have any experience at all. If they go thinking about Alice, grieving with her about her sad life, they feel her presence in a great way.

Fifteen Queens College students were taking an extracurricular course in ESP. They were told that if anyone could actually see an apparition it would be them because they were "tuned in" to ghosts.

Some of the students worried that the trip would not reveal a ghost and their time away from the campus would be wasted. The counselor said, "We'll enjoy the trip. It's so lovely today." I told the girls they could recognize Alice's grave by the flat marble slab with ALICE carved on it.

When they arrived at the gravesite, the students closed their eyes and walked backward around the grave thirteen times. After that, they became frightened and one of them said, "No one else is in the cemetery with us."

Just then a beautiful girl in a long white dress walked by.

"Where did *she* come from?" a student asked.

"It's Alice, the ghost!" another student screamed.

At that moment the girls realized they had seen the ghost of Alice Flagg—although, by then, Alice had disappeared. The girls and their counselor left the cemetery quickly and spent the night on Pawleys Island. The following day they returned to the cemetery to see if Alice would return. They arrived late in the day, about the same time they had seen Alice the day before. It worked. Alice was sitting on the wall that surrounds the cemetery, with her feet dangling.

Photograph by Sid Rhyne.

All of the girls except one, Mary, ran about twenty-five feet in the opposite direction. They called to Mary. "Come here with us. That's Alice, the ghost. Don't stay there." One student said, "Mary, for Heaven's sake, come here. You're standing too close to the ghost."

Mary walked slowly, her head high, her eyes looking into the distance, until she reached Alice's grave. She stopped.

"Come over here, Mary," a friend coaxed.

As Mary stood by the grave, Alice jumped from the wall and floated to her grave. She stood next to Mary. Mary extended a hand, but it went right through the apparition.

Alice, without making a sound, lifted off the ground and, in a horizontal position, as if sleeping, floated down into her burial place.

Mary fainted and fell atop the grave. Her friends ran to the old pumphouse and wet handkerchiefs to place on Mary's forehead. When they revived their friend, the sick girl began to speak in an unknown tongue. She didn't recover her normal mental health until she arrived home, in Charlotte.

That's exactly how it happened. There was no reason for those girls to come back here and tell me the story.

Hurricane Hugo crashed onto the Carolina shore in 1989, leaving millions of dollars of damaged property. In that same year a deep snow fell on Myrtle Beach and nearby islands at Christmas. A large snowfall is unusual for this part of the state. All this took place the very year Clarke A. Willcox died. The Hermitage was sold and moved from the property, leaving room for the upscale housing development that occupies that scenic space today.

Only the Sculptures of God

The defining moment of my writing career came on September 1, 1976, when I met Mrs. Genevieve Willcox Chandler, sister of Clarke A. Willcox. The gracious Mrs. Chandler was an artist, an extraordinary storyteller, and something of a barometer of historical hotspots on the South Carolina coast. She was born in Marion, South Carolina, but her father fell deeply in love with the seaside village of Murrells Inlet and moved to the Hermitage. It was at her own house, not the Hermitage, that I first met her. Mrs. Chandler's beautiful paintings of Low Country scenes graced her walls and were propped on the floorboards against the walls. I admired her for many reasons, not the least of which was her amazing memory.

> When I was a child, we had a house party at our home [the Hermitage] in Murrells Inlet. I and the other children decided to visit the Old Doctor [Dr. J. Ward Flagg, nephew of Dr. Allard Flagg

and his sister Alice] at his cottage at
Brookgreen Plantation and hear his narrative about the hurricane of 1893, locally
called the Flagg Flood.

That storm will always be remembered as one of the most
deadly in Low Country history. Mrs. Chandler said there were
eyewitness accounts of people falling from tree limbs into the
angry, churning waves during the hurricane. Dr. J. Ward
Flagg's strength and courage in hanging on to the tree limb

Archer M. Huntington talks with Dr. J. Ward Flagg on the steps of "the old
doctor's" cottage at Brookgreen. Photo courtesy of Brookgreen Gardens.

throughout the hours of violent weather spared his life.

Dr. Flagg was popular not only as a physician but as a storyteller. Many people of the South Carolina Low Country and beyond sought an audience with him. Genevieve and her friends who were attending the house party decided to do the same. Her mother, not sure how the children would be received by Dr. Flagg, was at first skeptical. Finally, she said, "Better an unpleasant adventure than no adventure at all." With that, she called old Isaac Smith who, in his black beard and great big straw hat, drove the two mules that pulled the wagon.

Mrs. Chandler settled down to enjoy telling me her story.

All the boys and girls were in their teens, and Mother crawled into the wagon with us. Before we reached Dr. Flagg's cottage, we went through a boggy place, which today is the Diana Pool at Brookgreen Gardens. We went up the avenue of magnificent oaks in our two-horse wagon.

Dr. Flagg, bereaved of family by the storm, lived in a cottage on his late grandfather's plantation, Brookgreen. He lived in the house with Uncle Tom

Duncan, his man of everything: chauffeur, companion, cook, friend. Dr. Flagg was surrounded by relics of the past, such as a beautiful old Indian ax that washed up on the beach after the hurricane. Other valuable artifacts were displayed in his cottage.

We hurriedly made up an excuse that one of the girls had sprained her ankle, using this pretext in case he was not disposed to accept a group of hearty teenagers. But we needn't have been concerned. He welcomed us with his booming voice, which echoed like thunder.

Oh, he fascinated us, telling us stories! We all listened to each word, our eyes as big as saucers as he told the story of the hurricane. With his luxuriant white beard, he could have passed as one of the old prophets. He looked like Moses.

The full force of the storm struck on a high tide at Murrells Inlet October 13, 1893, but there were ominous signs of a hurricane the night before. A gale-force wind rattled the beach cottages. Dr. Arthur Flagg, 65, and his wife, Georgeanna Ward Flagg, 60, were in their cottage with their son, Dr. J. Ward

Flagg, 33, three nieces, and several servants. During the night, J. Ward Flagg heard someone in the hallway say, "There must have been an earthquake at sea." His mother's voice came from her bedroom, saying, "Go back to bed. Put your faith in God."

Things were no better in the morning. The family took refuge in a cedar tree. When Dr. Arthur Flagg saw his wife loosen her grip, he embraced her. Dr. J. Ward Flagg tried to save them but they were gone. When the storm abated, Dr. J. Ward Flagg, one niece, a male friend, and five servants still clung to the tree.

Mrs. Chandler continued her story.

> After the storm, Dr. Flagg ministered to all who came to him, and he supplied medication free to those who couldn't pay for it. When he was buried, in 1938, spirituals were sung by two hundred black friends, the voices wafting on the soft breeze among the oaks. The governor came to the funeral.

Mrs. Chandler ended her narrative by saying that as the wagon left Brookgreen, they all knew they would never forget Dr. J. Ward Flagg.

We looked out at the oaks that night, not knowing that one day that place would become a garden setting for the world's largest collection of outdoor statuary. That night there were only the sculptures of God.

Herbert Spencer, the English philosopher, believed that sculpture could truly be called the efflorescence of life. So felt Genevieve Willcox Chandler, who again walks among the sculptures of God.

A Most Prized Possession

In 1930 Archer Milton Huntington, the son of one of the country's wealthiest men, bought four colonial estates on the Waccamaw River. For a millionaire to step off his private yacht, the *Rozinante*, during the Great Depression and buy four local plantations was an event of historical proportions, or so the poor people of the area believed.

The Huntingtons continued their voyage to the British West Indies, and when they were back in their home in New York, they decided to carve from the coastal South Carolina property an outdoor sculpture garden. They returned to Murrells Inlet and got to work. After a few years, the garden was opened to the public.

At the post office one day, Genevieve Willcox Chandler was told by the postmistress that Mr. Huntington was hiring someone to take charge of the information department at Brookgreen Gardens.

"I called on Mr. Huntington and asked for three minutes of his time," Mrs. Chandler said.

"Why not five minutes?" he asked.

Mrs. Chandler responded that her beautiful and youngest son, William, was with her. She proceeded to tell Huntington that she had come to apply for the job of taking care
of his information office and to provide local folklore. She
had for several years collected folklore of the area for John A.
Lomax of the Library of Congress. She knew most of the original settlers around Murrells Inlet, the fishermen, and African
American residents. Having taught school for twenty-five years
she knew most of the younger generation.

Needless to say, she got the job. Leaving the interview,
she asked her son Bill, "What did you think of him?" "Mama,
I think he's got the biggest foot I ever saw." Later they learned
that a horse had once stepped on Huntington's foot and no
treatment was given. He wore a size fourteen shoe.

The Huntingtons built a home for themselves on the
beach, which they named Atalaya. Mrs. Chandler was invited
to dine there.

> They had Scottish maids who spoke
> with heavy accents. There were also Scot-
> tish washerwomen. Every morning the
> Huntingtons had fresh linen sheets on
> their beds, which was a luxury none of
> the rest of us could afford. But it sounds
> nice, doesn't it? Mr. Huntington liked the

Scots and believed they were completely trustworthy.

Mrs. Huntington served very simple food at the dinner party. There were blocks of ice cream and a silver knife. You cut the amount of ice cream you wanted.

Today my most prized possession is a dining table and chairs that were in that dining room. Mrs. Huntington gave them to me when they moved away. It is the prettiest iron set, with a glass top at least three-quarters of an inch thick. It's in the parsonage at Murrells Inlet at the present time. I have the two arm chairs and six side chairs, and the sideboard that was against the wall.

The Huntingtons were among the wealthiest people in the country, and they frequently entertained. If one stops to think who might have dined at that table, it stuns the imagination. Of all the guests, however, surely the most extraordinary talent was Genevieve Willcox Chandler.

The Misspelled Word

On September 12, 1977, Genevieve Willcox Chandler sat down with me in her living room overlooking the creek in Murrells Inlet and told me about Archer Milton Huntington.

Mr. Huntington remembered everything he had ever seen or heard or written. I remember the day Miss Perkins, his secretary, arrived from New York. She was a tiny little woman, an efficiency expert. I never will forget the conversation that morning. I made some remark about the Song of Solomon being in the Apocrypha. Mr. Huntington said, "In the Apocrypha? Miss Perkins, get the Bible!" She got the Bible and turned to the Song of Solomon and gave it to me. I began to read, and it sounded like a modern novel. I never will forget.

Mr. Huntington always came to work

looking like a retired Scotch country
gentleman, in his knickers, his high socks,
and his leather shoes that had been made
in London. He would come in and sit in
a chair by my beautiful fire. I put on five
or six big oak logs. I was very extravagant
with wood. There's nothing I enjoy in the
world like an open fire. He would come
in during the morning and talk by the
hour, by the fire.

They were a marvelous couple. He
believed, as my precious mother believed,
that we learn from everybody we touch
and become a part of everybody we have
met. And he could talk with the hum-
blest.

Archer Huntington loved poetry. To recite it and tell it
well was a sure path to his pleasure, and there was no dispute
about his skill at writing it. He spent years laboring over a
translation of the Spanish composition *Poem of the Cid*. The
quiet atmosphere of Brookgreen inspired him to write poetry,
and he did so by an open fire. One day he wrote a verse about
Rocinante. The poem was engraved in stone and displayed in
a wall bordering one side of the garden. Just after the tablet

was placed in the wall, Huntington left for Texas. He had not reviewed the exhibit.

One morning while meandering through the garden observing the sculpture, a visitor read the poem and noticed a misspelled word. He reported it to Huntington's office. Miss Perkins phoned him in Texas and told him about the error.

To Archer Huntington, a misspelled word was a catastrophe. It was a double calamity when it concerned something connected with Don Quixote, his favorite fictional character,

Photograph by Sid Rhyne.

or Rozinante, Don Quixote's horse. "I shall send a stone carver from Texas to correct the error," he said.

The stone carver arrived at Brookgreen. It was pointed out that the word "Manchegan" had been carved without the "e". When Huntington returned to Brookgreen Gardens, there was only a faint discoloration that divulged the change in lettering of the poem, and it remains so to this day.

ROCINANTE

When truth outwears, and withered fact grows cold.
When knowledge stales with plundered wisdom's gold.
Come gather in the garden of delight.
And journey with the mock Manchegan Knight.
Here, in a curtained pleasance of the mind
The sumptuous cenotaph to honor find
Raised by the god of laughter; he who hears
May scarce discern his merriment for tears.

Can truth or history such beauty keep
As vast reality of visions deep?
Shall deeds of Caesar or Napoleon ring
More true than Don Quijote's vapouring
Hath winged Pegasus more nobly trod
Than Rocinante stumbling up to God?

                              Archer Milton Huntington

Walking in His Shoes

In the 1980s I called on Mr. T. N. Cox, the superintendent of Arcadia Plantation. Cox was a man of culture, a historian, a horticulturist, and much more. I had long looked forward to a conference with him.

During Mr. Cox's narrative he told the story about Mr. Huntington's gift of shoes. In my mind I had already named the story "Walking In His Shoes." I regret I was never in a position to send the story out for publication. Mr. Cox began by describing Mr. Huntington.

Archer Milton Huntington, the only child of Collis P. Huntington, who built the Central Pacific Railroad and owned other railroads as well as the Newport News Shipbuilding and Drydock Company, was immense in height and depth of mind, but he shrank away from driving an automobile.

One sunny afternoon in the 1930s, as he enjoyed the scenery of Brookgreen and I drove, we came upon a workman digging a ditch. Mr. Huntington asked me to stop the car. He got out, stretched all of his six-foot-five-inch frame and went over to the laborer. "What size shoes do you wear?"

The man threw down his shovel.

Huntington pointed to his own shoes and said, "Size fourteen." He looked upon it as something of a coincidence that the laborer's feet appeared to be about the same size as his. "Do you wear this size?"

The man nodded.

Mr. Huntington slapped him on the back. "You are one of the heartiest fellows I've seen around here. My shoes are hand-made in London, crafted from the finest leather in the world. I'm going to make you a present of some of my shoes. So look out for it."

Upon returning home, Mr. Huntington had a box of shoes packaged and delivered to the man's cabin near the river.

I decided to try to locate Small Huggins, the recipient of the shoes, and find out what it was like for a poor man to wear shoes handmade in London. Someone told me where the laborer lived.

Sid accompanied me to the man's house. Foliage and limbs brushed against the car as we made our way down the sandy path. If a roadway actually existed, there was no sign of it. After a few hundred yards, Sid stopped the car. "I'm turning around right here," he proclaimed. "If we break down, we won't be found for eight days." I convinced him to keep going.

Eventually we had to leave the car and travel the rest of the way on foot. We walked through all manner of blackwater lagoon and dark woodland. Without warning, the house broke into view.

As fate would have it, no one was at home. We sat on the steps and waited.

When we were about to give up hope, Small Huggins arrived. I told him I had come in search of him to hear the story of the gift of Mr. Huntington's shoes—which he was at that moment wearing.

A grin spread across the man's face and his voice rose in a foreign language—or so I thought. I soon realized he was speaking a form of Gullah, the language spoken by many of the descendants of early South Carolina sea island blacks. This was many years ago and I had not heard this dialect spoken. When I realized I would not be able to communicate with Mr. Huggins, I handed him a gift I'd brought and we left.

I could not help thinking of the unusual circumstances of the two men—Huntington and Huggins—and the influence the gift of the leather shoes had upon both lives. I would love to have heard the story from Small Huggins.

As I reviewed the transcripts of my interviews with Low Country prople, I realized I had interviewed another man who was the recipient of some of Mr. Huntington's shoes. I met Rufus Thompson on September 1, 1976. He began his narrative by talking about the Huntingtons.

> Oh, he was very nice. He talked easy [sparingly], but she talked more. He was nice and kindly. Baptist preachers used to go up there, and he do a lot for them. My 'nomination is Methodist. I work in the garden, cleaning statues with soap and water, and I work some for Missus Jenny Bee [Genevieve Chandler]. I didn't have much up-and-down with the boss [Huntington] because I was in the garden. Had to be there every day.

I got one pair of the shoes, the crepe sole shoe. Had to wear three pair of socks and more than that on the right foot to make it fit. I believe I could have worn more socks than that because I put all kinds of things in the shoes to fill them up.

Wife of Sam Moultrie can tell you about the clothes. Sam got all the clothes.

A Sandy Island Wedding

I refer to my first meeting with Mr. and Mrs. Edwin Fulton on September 17, 1977, as a divine event. Our visits to their house are among Sid's and my favorite memories. Mrs. Fulton remained a close friend until she died. Stories truly rang forth from the voice of the late Ed Fulton.

When I met them, the Fultons lived in the caretaker's cottage at Wachesaw Plantation. W. A. Kimbel bought Richmond Hill and Wachesaw Plantations. The house in which the Fultons lived was close to the plantation manor house, where the Kimbels lived during the winter months. Ed Fulton was a grand gentleman, an expert at cabinet making, a much-sought-after hunting guide, and a historian.

The people living on Brookgreen Plantation when it was purchased by the Huntingtons included the Fulton family. They resided in the caretaker's cottage there as well. The caretaker's cottage at Brookgreen is used today as the Garden's Small Sculpture Gallery.

Fulton had been the caretaker for the former owner of Brookgreen Plantation. He was fond of saying that rice was

Isaac Deas, the gateman at
the Great Dane Gate in
Brookgreen Gardens, during
the time of the Huntingtons.
Photo   courtesy   of
Brookgreen Gardens.

grown in the Brookgreen rice fields as late as 1920.

During the time the Fultons resided at Brookgreen, Isaac
Deas was gatekeeper, where the Great Dane Gate is located
today. Isaac's wife was Martha. Fulton was full of stories,
including some about Martha and Isaac Deas. But he began
his narrative by showing us a photograph of an engine and
wheel.

See that engine and wheel? The fly-
wheel was twelve feet high, and the en-

gine had a six-foot stroke on it. They ran
the rice mill with the engine. That was at
The Oaks Plantation, one of those bought
by Huntington.

After telling us all about rice production, Fulton shared
the story of a recent marriage on Sandy Island, one of the last
undeveloped spots along South Carolina's rapidly developing
coast. To this day there is no bridge to the island. Two hundred years ago, the 12,000-acre island in the Waccamaw River,
in Georgetown County, had been home to nine prosperous
rice-producing plantations. Only two rice planters, Capt.
William Percival Vaux and Dr. Edward Thomas Herriott, made
their home on Sandy Island. Others resided on the eastern
bank of the Waccamaw or the western bank of the Pee Dee
River.

Sandy Island is populated today by the descendants of enslaved Africans who worked the rice fields. Fulton also worked
those rice fields before Huntington bought the property.

An African-American named Abraham
Herriott worked for me at Brookgreen. I
called him the mayor of Sandy Island. His
word was just about absolute law. If he told
one of the Sandy Islanders to do something,

they pretty well did it.

There was another island in that vicinity called Silver Island—the Sandy Islanders called it Silvan Islant. I asked Ham to put a rice trunk [flood gate] on Silver Island. Laborers would open and close the gate, allowing the water to flood the fields on a high tide and go back out when the tide ebbed. I made a rule that I wouldn't pay any laborer in the rice fields until the tide covered it three times. As a test, I had them throw a little grass there and the tide would wash it all out.

Ham put this rice trunk on Silver Island and asked for his pay. I wouldn't pay him. Now for a rice trunk to work properly, it had to be perfectly straight. If it leaned, it would not work.

I didn't see Ham for a week. Then one day he came to see me. "Cap'n, you been to Silvan Islant?" I said, "Yes." "I know what's the matter with that trunk," he said. "I do too," I answered. "That trunk is triangular and it ought to be perpendicular," he said. I said, "That *is* the trouble, isn't it?"

Ham didn't have any education but
he was smart.

Fulton showed us a photograph of a wedding on Sandy
Island. The groom was Ham Herriott, wearing a suit and a
bow tie. The bride wore a white wedding dress, and she looked
to be anything but relaxed. Fulton described the event.

Ham said to me, "Tomorrow's Saturday and I want you there."

I took the boat, with my wife and Mrs.
Kimbel. When we pulled up to the dock,
another boat edged in beside us. The
preacher who would officiate was in the
boat. "Signan, you going to marry Ham?"
I asked. "Yes, sir." "Well, I want you to do
a better job than the other preacher did
at marrying him. The other man married
him where he wouldn't stay home at night.
I want you to marry him where he'll stay
home at night." All the people on the island attended the wedding.

The bride was a poor little thing and
scared to death. But it turned out she

wasn't too scared to make Ham stay home
at night.

The name of gatekeeper Isaac Deas came up several times
during Fulton's narrative.

> Old Isaac Deas was a slave under
> Joshua John Ward, who I was told had
> up to 3,000 slaves at one time. Ward was
> the king of the rice planter in the district
> and the master of Brookgreen Plantation.
> Abraham Herriott told me that. Isaac's
> wife was Martha, but he called her Marty.
> She said the buckra [white people] made
> her marry Isaac. The buckra told her she
> must have sixteen children. She wouldn't
> let Isaac go out at night. If he did, she
> locked him out. She did that many a time.

In the spring of 2003 my husband Sid and I attended
Sunday School and church service at the New Bethel Missionary Baptist Church on Sandy Island. Nine of us, including
the pastor, the Reverend Karon Jackson, left the mainland at
9:00AM on a Sunday morning. The church-owned pontoon
boat zoomed along, following an old Huntington-built canal

in the abandoned rice fields about a mile to the Waccamaw River.

Genevieve Chandler had explained the building of the canal to me. She interviewed Gabe Lance, a Sandy Island resident, for the WPA Writers Project. According to Gabe Lance, who had been born in slavery and was living on Mount Arena Plantation on the island the day freedom came, "Slavery people cut kennel [canal] and dig ditch and cut down woods and dig ditch through the raw woods."

The pontoon entered the Intracoastal Waterway (Waccamaw River) and continued for another mile across the deep channel to Sandy Island, where it docked beside the Prince Washington School boat, used by the Sandy Island children who attend public schools on the mainland. Prince Washington was a mayor of Sandy Island. We traveled from the dock to the church by van on a road the islanders call Highway 101. The white sandy road followed many curves, sand hills, and forests through Mount Arena Plantation. The islanders on the van told me they all get along perfectly with one another. "We call everybody on Sandy Island 'cousin'," one said. I found that to be true. Onethia Elliot, of Mount Arena, is the oldest person living on Sandy Island. Her comfortable home is surrounded by a well-kept flower garden.

Dr. Edward Thomas Heriot owned Mount Arena Plantation and lived there in 1850. Dr. Heriot's eldest son, Francis

Withers Heriot, succeeded his father as planter and made his home at Mount Arena. Gabe Lance described the day freedom came to the island.

> About ten o'clock in the morning, soldier all muster out of gunboats and scatter all over the island. Gun on shoulder glisten 'gainst the sun. Blue coats, blue pants, hat all blue. Some came back to the landing 'bout five o'clock. Have hog, geese, duck. Broke in barn. Stole rations from poor people. Maussa Frank Heriot gone in swamp. Hid in woods. My grandfather take Missus Sally Heriot on his back to hide 'em in the woods where Maussa was. Yankee stay but the one day. But it was Great Peace!

New Bethel Church inspires serenity, standing stoicly among the old island trees. The creamy white wood structure, which is surrounded by a fence, invites visitors from all walks of life. Among the island families who have worshipped here are the Herriotts. A plaque in the vestibule commemorates four Herriott children, all of whom drowned on the same day. Two boys went into the river and got into trouble. The girls went in to rescue them.

Windows in the church are inscribed with names of the families who contributed them. One inscription reads, "Deacon James Herriott and family." Other names include Pyatt, Tucker, and Elliott. Red-cushioned pews provide comfort for the worshipers.

The Sunday School teacher presented a well-prepared lesson and encouraged feedback from class attendees. At one point she said, "I knew a man who did not live right, but he knew the word of God. He knew the scripture from Genesis to Revelation. He didn't have to run home and refer to the Bible—he knew the scripture perfectly. But he was the cussingest man I ever was acquainted with." The lesson ended with a remarkable rendition of "Near The Cross," sung by class members.

The worship service began to the hand clapping of several women in the congregation to the tempo of the spiritual "Do Lord." Their voices followed in unison, "Do Lord, oh do Lord, oh do remember me," repeating the chorus many times.

The choir was made up of men wearing green jackets, black trousers, and white shirts and dark ties.

The minister stood at the podium in his white robe. The sermon, based on Romans 12:2, drew many Amens from the congregation and the spontaneous clapping of hands. Reverend Jackson's deep voice resounded through the small church.

Roses Without Thorns

Many times during the 1980s I interviewed George Young at his barbecue emporium on US 17 and at his home on Black River Road in Georgetown, South Carolina. He graciously gave of his time to tell me all I wanted to know—to give me the details of the connection of his family, descendants of slaves, to George Vanderbilt. This story begins when George was a little boy, growing up in a cabin on Arcadia Plantation.

In 1906 Isaac Emerson, of Baltimore, bought five adjoining Georgetown County plantations. He named them collectively Arcadia Plantation.

Mr. George Vanderbilt, a son of Margaret Emerson Vanderbilt, inherited Arcadia Plantation from his grandfather, Capt. Isaac Emerson, liked to see roses grow around the little houses that once were slave cabins. He established a tradition of giving a prize for the prettiest roses grown by a child from the cabins in the settlement. I had never won the prize. To do so was my fondest dream.

Mr. Vanderbilt called for the children to come to the stable. He told us to select some roses for planting. I noticed some long green shoots, grabbed an armful and flew home, where I planted them neatly in rows.

A few weeks later, Mr. Vanderbilt called on the children and asked to see the roses. It was not yet time for them to bloom, and Mr. Vanderbilt was not ready to award the prize. He wanted to see what degree of progress we children were making.

We gathered around the wealthy man and followed him from one house to another. I could hardly wait for Mr. Vanderbilt to see how my roses had grown. Finally, the riffraff army reached my house. When the master of the plantation gazed at my plants, I held my breath. I was nervous as I awaited the acknowledgment of what I hoped were the best roses.

"Why, George," said Vanderbilt.

"Yes, sir?"

"They are not roses. They are onions."

Mr. Vanderbilt looked at me. It was clear I was heartbroken.

"I've viewed all the vegetable gardens on this plantation," he said. "And I haven't seen any onions that compare to these. Yours are larger, greener, and finer than any other. When the day comes that I award the prize for the finest roses, bring your onions and enter them in the competition."

"Yes, sir."

The day came. George Young carried his bundle of onions into the stable. He looked around. What fanciful beauty! Vivid reds, pinks, whites, and yellows. It was beyond doubt that a display of roses would win the prize.

Vanderbilt gave a little speech and awarded the prize for the finest roses to George Young for his onions. The plantation owner said he had never seen such big onions. From that day on, George Young found a faithful haven in the friendship of George Vanderbilt. He became Vanderbilt's butler and traveled the world with him.

The Best of the Hunting Dogs

George Young's father helped take care of the Arcadia Plantation hunting dogs. The most prized dog was Lambkin.

Hunting rituals changed little from Isaac Emerson's time to the Vanderbilt days, except that in Emerson's time the dogs were carried to the scene of the hunt in a wagon pulled by horses. In Vanderbilt's time they rode in pickups. When the hunters were ready to chase a fox, the man in charge of the dogs put out two that were the best at tracking. The rest of the pack remained in the truck. When the tracking dogs barked, indicating they had picked up the trail of a fox, the rest of the pack was let out to join the chase. The hounds ran through the forests and up and down the sand dunes, and the hunters on their horses kept up with them as best they could. George Young, his father, and T. N. Cox acted as hunting guides. One hunt stood out in George Young's mind.

We had Lambkin in the back of the truck with all the other dogs, waiting for the trackers to pick up the scent of a fox.

Suddenly a fox was spotted. "Turn Lambkin out," Mr. Cox yelled. I tell you the truth, Lambkin ran so fast after that fox we were worried about him.

The hunters screamed in delight when they recognized the yelps of their own dogs, but our thoughts were on Lambkin. Lambkin ran as fast as a bullet for about thirty minutes, and then something happened. I got out of the truck and ran to him. Lambkin had run so fast he ran into a tree and killed himself. He was a dead dog. We were so sorry to lose Lambkin. There never was a match to him. He was the best of all of Arcadia's hunting dogs.

Baruch's Place

Hobcaw Barony, it is said, began as one of ten baronies of 12,000 acres each, laid out in 1711 and divided among the Lords Proprietors by lot. The land was divided again and again before Wall Street financier Bernard M. Baruch came into ownership of most of it about the beginning of the twentieth century. Well hidden in forests, swamps, and coves, it was the perfect place for pirates to hide their loot. Hollywood couldn't have produced a better set.

The name says it all. Hobcaw Barony, an Indian name, means "between the waters."

The original house used by the Baruchs, Friendfield Plantation manor house, burned to the ground on Christmas Eve, 1929. The next year Baruch built a mansion overlooking Winyah Bay. Although he became seasick at the thought of traveling by water, he built a dock downhill from the front porch of the mansion and kept a fleet of boats there.

My first interview about Hobcaw was with Olive Buxton Mancill, a Georgetown school teacher who had been brought up on the plantation. Her father, Cap'n. Buxton, as he was called by everyone, was Baruch's yachtsman. Her mother was the plantation school teacher. Olive devoted an entire day to me, meeting Sid and me at Hobcaw on June 29, 1977.

Mrs. Woodrow Wilson visited Hobcaw several times after World War I and again for rest and recuperation during the time right after President Wilson's death. I was asked over to the big house several times during Mrs. Wilson's visits. I was told later that Mrs. Wilson had requested the company of a young person. I was probably six or seven years old at the time. We played cards and she taught me several card tricks.

Mr. Baruch had *Kaymore*, a yacht; *Eagle Point*; a freight boat called *Sea Dog*; and *Chick*, a very fast boat named by his children, who called their father Chick.

Hobcaw was filled with wild creatures. You could hear the alligators bellow at dawn. If an alligator was hungry, he would attack anything that fell into the water, including a child or a dog. An alligator could handle big servings.

The dock was much wider than it is now and the *Eagle Point* was docked at the end of the pier. I spent many hours up near the house, watching snakes slither over and under the rocks piled up to protect the dock area from high, stormy waters. Sometimes I walked from the bulkhead rocks to the boathouse, where boats were hauled to be repaired. I saw snakes and alligators almost every time.

There was no bridge across Winyah Bay then and I rode the ferry to go to school. The names of the ferries were *Pelican* and *Cornwallis*. My father worked for Mr. Baruch on his boats up in New York and Long Island, and we went there in the summertime. We all looked forward to coming back here in the fall to escape the cold weather up there. Mr. Baruch wore knickers and caps with bibs. I remember him with a big gray cape swinging around his shoulders. My father wore a uniform.

There was a house on the plantation called Clambank where the duck hunters spent the night. The decoys and guns were kept there.

My Christmas tree always came by rowboat because the cedar trees grown on the rice field banks were round and beautiful. My parents decorated the tree. I never saw it until Christmas morning. It was lighted with real candles.

Mr. Baruch never carried any money with him. When he saw something he wanted, he called, "Buck." My father added that to his expense account.

Olive Mancill and the quaint and interesting ways of her upbringing are gone. Her son, who owns a thriving electrical and plumbing business in Myrtle Beach, carries on the family name.

Deary-Deer

Miss Ella Severin, the late Belle Baruch's companion, agreed to an interview for the fall of 1989, but we set no date. I received a note dated July 23, 1989, from Miss Severin advising me that she would be in France in August. She wrote from France, saying she looked forward to our conference. When she returned to South Carolina, she contacted me to set a date.

Sid and I traveled to Bellefield Plantation on the agreed date. Miss Severin sent her chauffeur, Princey Jenkins, to meet us at the plantation gate. Sid and I would never have found our way to the house on the eighty miles of roadways networking the plantation.

Belle's graceful home was like a drama in two acts. To get to the residence we drove through the barn, where some of the hundreds of trophies awarded Belle Baruch for her equestrian and sailing abilities are displayed. Among the trophies was a plaque from the Queen of the Bay Cup, a New York regatta. When I could pull my eyes away from the multitude of prizes on display, I examined the building, a design as brilliant as it was simple. Eight stalls lined the walls for Belle's thoroughbred horses.

Exiting the barn, we were in the yard of Belle's house, built in 1936. She was in France when her house was constructed, but she supervised the building of the barn.

Miss Severin met us at the door and led us into the living room. Our eyes were immediately drawn to the large painting of Belle astride *Souriant*, her favorite horse. We settled down in the den, a room perfectly fit for a hunting lodge—exposed

Belle Baruch's stable. The road leading to Bellefield House goes through this door, and as one passes through, hundreds of Belle's trophies are seen on the walls of the stable. Belle kept her famous horses, including Souriant, here. Photograph by Sid Rhyne.

beams, floors of old brick, large fireplace, and stuffed wild-cats and other wildlife. I noticed a framed snapshot of a small deer that obviously had the run of the house. Deary-Deer was written on the photo.

Miss Severin began her story.

> Mr. Baruch settled a large amount of money on each of his children. Belle did not use her money for an education as he expected, but, instead, she financed a se-ries of winter excursions to southern France, where she studied horses and riding and finally purchased the beauti-ful Anglo-Arab horse named Souriant. Belle hired a French groom to train Souriant. This magnificent animal won many tro-phies and was the envy of Europe.
>
> In 1931 Belle received the *La Coupe du president* [French President's Cup] for winning the classic competition in the Paris horse show. Belle was the only one of 119 contestants, including French cav-alry officers, to make a perfect score. Her trophy was a *Sevres* porcelain that she re-ferred to as a mid-Victorian eyesore.

It was in Paris that Belle met Miss Severin, who would remain a friend for life.

Leaving the house late in the day Sid and I noticed in the yard, between the residence and the stable, a white fence under a huge oak tree. A plaque attached to the oak marked the final resting place of Belle's beloved Souriant:

Souriant

"Toto"

Anglo-Arab

France, 1923 to June 25, 1956

My gallant horse and faithful friend

Adieu

My day with Miss Severin at Bellefield remained vivid in my memory and I thought of Belle Baruch often. During 2002, Lee Brockington, a pillar of Hobcaw Barony as well as the South Carolina Low County, invited Sid and me to ride along as she toured the plantation with a descendant of a Hobcaw slave family.

Lee maneuvered the van slowly through the dense woods. Suddenly, ahead of us a small silhouette appeared against the green backdrop of brush. Lee brought the van to a stop and shut off the engine. As we watched in breathless silence, a wee deer, no larger than a cat, made a grand effort to stand

Painting of Belle Baruch on Souriant by Alfred J. Munnings. Photo courtesy of Miss Ella Severin.

upright on wobbly legs. The mother deer was nowhere in sight.

My heart ached for this tiny creature all alone in the woods. I thought about Belle Baruch's Deary Deer, the abandoned fawn she raised in her home. What a privilege it would have been to adopt the down-soft little deer and save it from predators like the feral hogs that roam the Hobcaw woods.

Lee called the Hobcaw Visitors Center, gave the location of the baby deer, and asked that someone check on the animal. As she started the van and began to move forward, I realized my arms were outstretched as if to cuddle and comfort the new baby.

The little "Deary-Deer" lying in the leaves, its big brown eyes newly opened, looked for all the world like a child's stuffed toy. As we drove out of sight, I looked back and thought of all the adventures this little fellow would have growing up on Hobcaw. I felt certain the fawn would be rescued in time. This gave me comfort.

The Nurse
Who Went Hunting

On June 19, 1991, Sid and I drove to Kingstree, South
Carolina, to interview Miss Elizabeth Navarro, who served as
Bernard Baruch's nurse for twenty-eight years, from shortly
after World War II until his death in 1965. Driving through
the countryside, just outside town, we noticed a sign that read
"Little Hobcaw." We stopped the car to take in the view: a
palatial white home stood at the end of a long avenue of trees.
When Baruch decided to spend the rest of his days hunting
quail, he built this country house for his nurse. After his death,
she sold it and moved into Kingstree.

Elizabeth Navarro was a petite, handsome blond about
seventy. We sat in the living room of her large ranch-style,
brick home—which was gracious, but no match for the Baruch
home on Fifth Avenue, Hobcaw Barony in Georgetown
County, or Little Hobcaw. The one-story Kingstree house was
grandly furnished. Navarro pointed out two mahogany tables
with piecrust tops, which is to say each had a top with scal-
loped molding. "These tables came from the Baruchs' New

York home," she explained. "An antiques dealer told me they are the most valuable things I own." Navarro directed our attention to the dining room. "The table and chairs in there are some of my best things." A quick glance revealed the grandeur of the table and chairs. Here and there about the house lay trappings of the swells, even nobility. I asked about her beautiful needlework pillows and discovered that she had embroidered them.

"Have you had quail lately?" Navarro asked, changing the subject. "No?" She called to her housekeeper, "Julia, bring a package of four quail from the freezer." The people who bought

Bernard Baruch and Elizabeth Navarro. Photo courtesy of Miss Elizabeth Navarro.

Little Hobcaw kept Navarro supplied with quail brought down in the fields where she and Bernard Baruch hunted for many years.

We continued our tour.

The hallway was a small gallery of sorts. Both walls were hung with framed photographs of people I couldn't resist asking about: Churchills; Roosevelts; people from show business, like Arthur Godfrey; and the cream of society—the Vanity Fair set. Navarro directed me to open the door to the hall closet. I almost gasped when I did so, for my eyes were met by a row of the most magnificent furs I had ever beheld.

Although I was drooling and anxious to see more, the time had come to settle down and hear her story.

> Churchill and those people didn't know beans about hunting. Mr. Baruch had a walk built from his porch at Hobcaw House down the hill to the dock. They took a few boat rides, but mostly they sat on the porch and talked about politics.
>
> After World War II, when the atmosphere in Washington was tense, Gen. George Marshall, on whom Truman depended for judgment, called and asked if he could fly to Hobcaw and talk with Mr.

Baruch. We had a wonderful time with
General Marshall.

Mr. Baruch kept in constant touch
with his secretary, Miss Boyle. She never
came down to Hobcaw as far as I know,
but she ran Mr. Baruch's New York office
as well as he could have run it. She was
perfectly loyal to him and he appreciated
that. He showed his appreciation in many
ways. She had an ermine coat.

We had an old Chevrolet at Hobcaw
and I drove Mr. Baruch to Georgetown
every morning. A bridge had been built
over Winyah Bay. In Georgetown Mr.
Baruch found out what the stock market
was doing. He called Miss Boyle after that.
I always drove him everywhere. He never
touched a steering wheel, at least after I
came to work for him.

Mr. Baruch hunted ducks in the earlier days, but his passion was going into
the open fields on a horse. When he decided that Hobcaw was too heavily wooded
and had few open fields suited to quail

hunting, he turned all of that huge estate over to his daughter, Belle, and bought a large tract of land near Kingstree. Dave McGill was his superintendent. He took care of the horses. Princey drove us and we went to Kingstree every day except Sunday. Mr. Baruch believed that shooting on Sunday was irreverent to his Christian friends in the Low Country.

After Mr. Baruch sent me to Abercrombie & Fitch in New York for my hunting clothes and instruction in shooting, I hunted every day with him when the season was open and it was not raining. It wasn't long before I bagged my allotment. Fifteen birds a day was the limit. No one dared come home without killing the allotted number of quail. Hunting quail was Mr. Baruch's favorite pastime.

Little Hobcaw

My next interview with Miss Elizabeth Navarro was at her home in Kingstree, South Carolina, on November 13, 1991. She began her narrative with, "Mr. Baruch said, 'I'm going to build you a house.'" She knew instinctively it would be on the Kingstree property. "'I don't want a big house,' I told him, 'but I want a nice house and some servants to help me keep it up.' He built a lovely house. Everybody who walked in thought it was charming."

Although Little Hobcaw was filled with amenities of the day, including an indoor, heated pool, the house looked as though it could had been there a hundred years. Except for small dinner parties, which always included quail, Baruch and Navarro lived quietly at Little Hobcaw. T. N. Cox, of Arcadia Plantation, assisted Navarro in designing the camellia gardens. Baruch told Cox to provide her with as many camellias as she wanted because they were winning prizes.

T. N. Cox opened a nursery on U.S. Highway 17 at Arcadia Plantation and became an expert at growing camellias. He joined the American Camellia Society and his blooms won many awards. People from other states drove to Georgetown to buy camellias at Little Red Barn Nursery.

This was a special time in Navarro's life.

> Mr. Baruch did not go back to Hobcaw after Belle took it over. He had all the land and property he wanted in Kingstree and he didn't want the responsibility of the plantation. He loved it over here.
>
> He did not get up early but had breakfast in bed: a soft-boiled egg, coffee, and one piece of toast. Lunch consisted of chicken. He did not have a big appetite. He had one drink of bourbon before dinner. He went to bed at ten o'clock on the dot, then got up after a couple of hours and sat in a straight chair. We played cards the rest of the night.
>
> My life was a miracle in many ways. I first met Mr. Baruch through the Broadway producer Billy Rose. I was attending a party at Rose's house. He said he had a friend who was looking for a nurse. I arrived at Mr. Baruch's office for my inter-

view and he grilled me with questions. I explained that I had graduated from Baltimore General Hospital and received the highest grade of any nurse in Maryland. He told me to come to work the next day.

Every time Mr. Baruch and I went to London we stayed at the Churchills' house. Sir Winston had a barn full of his own paintings. He sent me one before he died. It was hanging at Little Hobcaw when a doctor from Columbia wanted to buy it for $7,000. I had to pay more than that in taxes.

Mr. Baruch was a shrewd businessman. I didn't look at things the way he did. One day he and I went for a ride in the country around Little Hobcaw. We stopped at a grocery store. Mr. Baruch picked up four pieces of candy. I pointed out that it was a better deal to get a full package. "It's not a better deal if you don't want more than four pieces," he said.

Mr. Baruch could do anything. One day before we moved over here, he returned to Hobcaw Barony from Washington. He went into the kitchen and was

going over a list of arduous tasks the president had given him. He was advisor to
seven presidents, you know. As he labored
over the list, the cook just shook her head
and said, "May Jesus prop him up."

Elizabeth Navarro lived until her death in her comfortable, ranch-style home in Kingstree, South Carolina. I think
of her often and feel deep gratitude for the time she gave me
and the stories she shared.

The Origin of
She Crab Soup

Sue Alston lived in a house on a sandy lane—"the one less traveled by," Robert Frost might have said. The small residence had been constructed for her by Archibald Rutledge, South Carolina's first poet laureate and the last in the long line of Rutledges to own Hampton Plantation, between Georgetown and Charleston. The Hampton mansion was little more than a stone's throw from Sue's house. From her porch, her corncob pipe in her mouth, Sue preached the doctrines and recounted the stories told her by "Me ole Missus," Margaret Hamilton Seabrook Rutledge, Archibald's mother. Sue usually started her narrative with a tale about a Pinckney or a Rutledge, aristocratic and historic families who played important roles in the early days of the state of South Carolina and Hampton Plantation.

You remember that old story 'bout
Missus Harriott Horry of Hampton Plantation a-marrying Marse Fred Rutledge of

Charleston, a son of John Rutledge? Well, that was the first begin of the Rutledge at Hampton. Oh, that was a happy-hearted day when Missus Harriott marry a son of John Rutledge. That was something.

Marse John Rutledge owned that big ole mansion on Broad Street. Just like I was the cook in the Hampton kitchen, what be a separate building, a little ways off from the big house, Marse John Rutledge had a cook at his Charleston mansion, a building away from the big house, and that be where the She Crab Soup originate. Yes, ma'am, I tell it just like it happen yesterday. Marse John Rutledge was a man on his feet.

John Rutledge, son of Dr. John Rutledge and Sarah Hext Rutledge, was born in 1739 and studied law in the Court Temple in London. Wealthy South Carolinians in pre-Revolutionary days sent their sons to England to be educated, and in spite of the fact that his father died when John was only ten years old, he completed his education at Temple Bar. Family records show that $3,000 a year was required to complete Rutledge's legal education in London. When he became a full fledged barrister, his cap and gown cost an additional $250. He returned to Charles Town in 1761 at the age of twenty-two to begin his career as a lawyer. The next year he was elected to the Provincial Assembly and quickly became a strong voice in opposing what he considered unwarrantable interference of the Royal Governor in matters of election.

On May 1, 1763, Rutledge married Elizabeth Grimke. The wedding was small for people of their social standing. No guests were invited. The vows were heard by the rector in St. Phillips Church with two of the rector's servants as witnesses. The marriage produced ten children. Elizabeth was aunt to the famous Charleston abolitionist Grimke sisters.

In 1764, Rutledge became attorney general pro tempore of South Carolina, holding this position until June 1765, when he became a delegate to the Colonial Congress, which had assembled upon passage of the Stamp Act.

Rutledge was a delegate to the first Continental Congress in 1774, and in 1775 he joined John Adams in advocating a complete separation from the mother country. Rutledge's strong voice gained him popularity and won him the reputation of being the most effective speaker on the floor. Patrick Henry believed him to be the greatest orator in the congressional body and had proclaimed him as such from the time of his maiden speech.

In 1776 Rutledge was elected president of South Carolina

under the independent constitution. With the threat of British forces approaching the colony, Rutledge rallied 6,000 men and erected Fort Moultrie to protect the state. After the Declaration of Independence was created, he refused to ratify the new state constitution and resigned his office in March

The Rutledge House. The pre-Revolution mansion at 116 Broad Street is a fine example of a residence designed to be used for official functions. She Crab Soup originated in the kitchen. Photograph by Sid Rhyne.

1778. However, upon the second invasion of the British in February 1779, he was recalled and invested with the powers of the highest post in the state, becoming South Carolina's first governor.

When his gubernatorial term expired, Rutledge was by law not eligible for re-election. Again he was sent to Congress.

As the years passed, Rutledge was made chancellor of South Carolina and declined the seat of judge of the federal court. In 1787 he was a member of the convention that framed the U.S. constitution. Rutledge went on to be appointed an associate justice of the Supreme Court.

The Rutledge home was built in 1760 at 116 Broad Street in Charles Town. It sported a ballroom that occupied the entire front of the second floor. The house's most elaborate feature is perhaps the ironwork on the front, dating back to 1853, when P.H. Hammarskold added balconies, fences, and stair rails. The ironwork was created by Christopher Werner, one of Charleston's most dedicated craftsmen. The Rutledge house enjoyed many honors, as did its owner, not the least of which is the discovery of She Crab Soup. Sue Alston knew a thing or two about that.

Missus, when the cook be asked to
"dress up" the drab beige crab chowder,
he look around for something to give the

Sue Alston. Photograph by
Sid Rhyne.

soup some color. He look first at the ole
he crab. Nothing 'bout him have any
color. Then he take a glance at the she
crab. Now the female crab have eggs in
her, and those eggs be orange-tinted crab
eggs. The cook remove the eggs and add
them to the pot. Not only did the eggs
improve the flavor but they gave the soup
a creamy yellow color. They dyed the
chowder, and from that day to this the
name of the chowder be She Crab Soup.

John Rutledge died in Charleston on January 14, 1800,
and was buried in St. Michael's churchyard. A small marble
slab, containing only his name and the dates of his birth and
death, is said to be according to his expressed wishes.

Sue Alston died in 1983 at the age of 110. She is buried at Hampton Plantation. Though she no longer rocks on the porch of her cabin, smoking her corncob pipe, I can still see her as plain as day—large loop earrings hanging from her ears, a colorful kerchief wound tight around her head, a cup of coffee balanced on her knee. "Come on over here," she said to me when we first met. "I tell you what I can't forgot!"

God bless you, Sue.

Healing George Washington's Horse

On February 13, 1985, I sat on the steps of Hampton house with Will Alston, Sue's son, who was by then an elderly man. Will shared Sue's deep interest in the history of his family and Hampton Plantation. He talked in the manner of his mother except he usually started a tale with the beginning of *his* ancestors—rather than the Rutledges—even when the story concerned George Washington.

It be like this, Missus. Old man Morris Alston, my great-grandfather, be the first of my line to come to Hampton Plantation. That be during slavery time. See zackly how far they come from? See where the Alston start? Old man Morris clear the land for the rice fields in the delta 'tween the North Santee and South Santee Rivers. He also help build a logging railroad that extend from Hampton all the way to Moncks Corner. Now his son, Will Alston, my grandfather—I be his namesake, you know—be born at Hampton. Right here. Right here.

Missus, you know the Pinckney? Well Marse Daniel Horry, he marry Missus Harriott Pinckney and they be the Marse and Missus of this place, right here. Now one of Missus Harriott's cousins was Marse Charles Pinckney, who be governor of South Carolina from 1789 to 1792. Pinckney serve four terms as governor of South Carolina and his first term be right when General Washington came to Hampton. He visit Columbia and Charleston too.

Dr. Rutledge like to talk 'bout that time when George Washington visit Hampton. Oh, man, General George Washington, a-standing on these steps right here where we sit now. And he go in and have a nice meal right there in the house.

On Monday, May 2, 1791, this notice appeared in the Charleston *City Gazette*: "From undoubted authority we learn that the President of the United States was in Georgetown on the 30th and was to dine yesterday at Mrs. Horry's. That he intends being in town this day at one o'clock and dine in a private manner with his Excellency, the Governor."

Though Governor Pinckney maintain a mansion at 16 Meeting Street in Charleston, he built a large home on lands in the fork of the Congaree and Wateree Rivers near East Granby. He call the place Mount Tacitus, which mean Quiet Hill.

When George Washington visit Columbia, he made a stop at Mount Tacitus, and a story went 'round 'bout that. General Washington's horse came down with the bots. He was laying down in the stable just like any horse when he's got the bots. When the white folks all gone into the house, a stable boy lay his hands on the horse and stroke him from the root of the tail to the tip of the nose. Then he pray, "In the name of the Father, the Son, and Holy Ghost, Amen."

When he open his eyes, there was General Washington, a-standing with his hat off. 'Bout an hour later, the horse got up, shook himself and walk to the tub. Then he walk over to the rack and took a bite of hay.

General Washington said, "Now that my horse is well I must start on my journey by daylight in the morning."

Will Alston passed away a while back. He knew the history of the plantation and even the horses. He spoke of a happy life at Hampton. "The boss [Archibald Rutledge] came along and scoop me up and off we flew on his stallion," he said. "We did that many a time." Will liked to do things the old fashioned way. He probably knew how to treat a horse sick with the bots.

Will Alston.
Photograph by Sid Rhyne.

The Charleston Jazzmen

Sarah Finley Dowling was in the yard when I arrived at her home on Bonds Avenue in Charleston, Thursday, March 16, 1995. Her hair was just turning silver around her dark handsome face. Wearing a long, slender skirt and low-heeled shoes, she was right in style.

Her house wasn't a great one like the mansions of the Charleston blue bloods she had known. It was a small, cozy cottage. Scrapbooks, newspaper clippings, letters, and other mementos of Daniel Joseph Jenkins, his orphanage and its bands, were spread over the tables in the living room. She went right to the heart of her narrative.

I knew Parson Jenkins well. When I went to work for him at the Jenkins Orphanage in 1931, I was paid ten dollars a month. Even ten dollars was money then, back in the thirties. I lived on Tradd Street. To my way of thinking, Charleston wasn't segregated then. Some of the blue bloods

lived in my block. I knew them well.
Sammy Smalls, a fish monger who moved
about in a goat cart and was DuBose
Heyward's inspiration for his book *Porgy*,
lived down on the end, at East Bay. I lived
on the other end of Tradd Street, at 149,
but I knew Sammy, down there on Cabbage Row.

Back then, Tradd Street was in Charleston's fashionable
section of town, "South of Broad [Street]," as it was called. It
offered a spectrum of stately homes, although most were not
well-kept during that time. Paint was peeling but the Charlestonians kept up their appearances as best they could. A servant girl shelling peas in a dishpan while she sat on the piazza
of an old mansion was a common sight.

Although Sarah had known the Jenkins family and was a
frequent visitor to the Jenkins Orphanage, the letters, scrapbooks, and clippings spread about the room offered me a con-
crete history of the orphanage before her arrival there.

Jenkins came to Charleston as a young lumberman and
lived on King Street, north of Broad. He was married to Lena
James and they had started their family. On December 16,
1891, while working on a consignment of lumber, he found
four half-frozen, half-dead waifs huddled together in a rail-

road boxcar. Their names were Herbert White, Edwin Curtis, James Andrews, and Jesse Moore. Through their circumstances Jenkins believed Providence was speaking, telling him to open

The four original boys with Reverend and Mrs. Jenkins. From the Collections of the Avery Research Center for African American History & Culture, College of Charleston, Charleston, South Carolina.

an orphanage for the poor and destitute children of Charleston, not only the four that came to his attention, but the multitude of others yet to be rescued.

Jenkins came to believe it would be necessary for him to find a rich native Charlestonian willing to stand up for him. He decided he would face Maj. Augustine Smythe, one of the most distinguished of the blue bloods. Smythe, a respected lawyer, lived at 31 Legare Street. Jenkins had heard bits and pieces of Major Smythe's history. Born on October 5, 1842, Smythe was son of the pastor of Second Presbyterian Church. His mother was a daughter of James Adger, a prominent city merchant. It was said that Major Smythe could turn out more work in a day than any other lawyer could complete in a week. Jenkins was a humble laborer, but he felt up to the task of meeting Smythe.

Parson Jenkins stood well over six feet tall, though slightly stoop-shouldered. He was neatly dressed with carefully-trimmed black hair and beard. He was a proud man. His voice was deep and resonant and he possessed a well-crafted vocabulary. When asked to do so, he accepted the call to serve as pastor of New Tabernacle Fourth Baptist Church on Palmetto Street.

Jenkins told Smythe he desired to open an orphanage. If he had found four needy children, there must be hundreds of others waiting to be rescued. He suggested the people of the city search their attics and donate musical instruments to the cause. Some black children had died of consumption of the lungs, sometimes called tuberculosis. That condition might be improved by the blowing of horns. If instruments could be rounded up, he would find a music teacher and pay the teacher's salary from his meager timber earnings.

It worked. Major Smythe said the people of Charleston would respond to the plea for aid.

Back at his shack, nestled in oleander, azalea, and palmetto at 660 King Street, Jenkins realized how far he had come. He chose Orphan Aid Society as the official fund name for collecting monies for the children's home.

The next year, on July 21, 1892, a charter to the Orphan Aid Society was granted. Jenkins would remember that year most fondly as the one in which Major Smythe secured use of the old maritime building at 20 Franklin Street, next to the city jail, for the orphanage. A two-story house next door was designated as living quarters for the Jenkinses.

Starting at this point in the history of the orphanage, Sarah suffused the Jenkins story with the life and spirit of the time.

> Parson spent every minute that he was
> not at the orphanage or in church in
> search of boys between the ages of five and

fifteen. Officers from the police department surrendered boys who had been ar-
rested for thievery and other offenses.
Requests poured in for young people aged
three to twenty-three, but Parson's discre-
tion ruled only those between five and fifteen as eligible. When each child was admitted, the secretary recorded the information in a large leather book. Her thin,
spidery script noted where each orphan
came from, usually "The Police" or "Po-

Jenkins Orphanage Building, Franklin Street. Photograph by Sid Rhyne.

lice Court," and any fine that was paid.

With Major Smythe's help, an advisory board was established: George W. Williams, president of Carolina Savings Bank; F. H. Frost, attorney at law; and Dr. F. L. Parker, dean of Carolina College. Dr. Parker was instrumental in Parson's ability to hire excellent teachers. Curriculum consisted of Bible reading, orthography, reading, arithmetic, word analysis, penmanship, geography, history, grammar, physiology, drawing, vocal and instrumental music, domestic economy, and religious training. Twelve noon each day was set aside for prayer meeting in the chapel on the second floor.

Lena did not want the Jenkins children to be considered orphans. She enrolled them at Avery Institute, a private school for black children founded by the American Missionary Association and Quakers. I too attended Avery.

Parson Jenkins hired two music teachers, P. M. "Hatsie" Logan and Francis Eugene Mikell. Only Parson made the

decision of which orphans were selected
for band practice. The conductor was just
as important to the success of the band as
the musicians, and there was one student
perfectly suited for that role—little Jesse
Moore. It wasn't long before Parson had
a band. Uniforms with brass buttons, pat-
terned after the current style of military
uniforms, were donated by the Citadel,
South Carolina's military college. Jesse's
uniform was slightly large for him, but
Parson liked the look it gave the small
band leader, making him appear even ti-
nier.

No advance notice was given with re-
spect to the band's first public appearance.
Band members were lined up on the
street. Jesse was in front of the trombones,
and other instruments followed. He lifted
his baton. When it came down, the troop
began to march. Parson could scarcely believe his ears. The sounds drifted into the
alleys, private gardens, and every nook and
cranny downtown. Someone yelled, "Here
Comes Jenkins." Spectators gathered, and

some of them threw money toward the band members. Parson quickly collected it and dropped the donations into his hat. *Now listen to me!* Some of the band members didn't like that at all. They felt the money was meant for them.

Everything ran well. The building was spotlessly clean. The orphans did all the work—scouring floors, making beds, taking care of the garden, and doing the laun-

Jenkins Orphanage Band; Jabbo Smith Papers. Courtesy of The South Caroliniana Library.

dry. They enrolled in regular classes and attended church every Sunday morning.

But Parson needed more money. He decided to print some circulars inviting Charleston citizens to a party. What started as a simple idea resulted in the First Annual Prize Fair of the Colored Orphanage, held at 20 Franklin Street. Posters were printed, circulars distributed all over town, and in schools. The First Annual Prize Fair was a success.

In 1895 the orphanage had an enrollment of more than five hundred, a staff of eight teachers and two laborers, all of whom shared the premises on Franklin. And then the storm of '95 descended on the land. Parson calmed everybody as best he could. After four hours of terror, the storm slacked off. The orphanage was wrecked. When damage was tallied, the debt came to nearly $2,000. That was a whole lot of money back then. Parson didn't know what to do but he knew which way to turn—toward Major Smythe's office.

Smythe suggested Parson Jenkins take his band to New York and play on street corners. If the people of Charleston threw coins to the musicians, New Yorkers likely would throw a wad. Smythe said his client, the Clyde Line Steamship Company, would reduce rates for the orphans.

The band arrived in New York. No spectators slowed their pace to listen to the music. Parson's hat was empty and the trip cleaned up his money.

Back in Charleston, he called on Major Smythe who suggested Parson take his band to London, where his hat would likely not be ample for the funds he would receive. Thirteen band members were selected for the trip. Uniforms were cleaned, band instruments polished, and the musicians given instruction about traveling in a foreign country.

On a street in the crowded central area of London, the band leader stepped out and raised his baton. People paused to take in the sight and sound. A policeman asked what they were doing. Parson explained they were from America. The officer pointed to the jammed-up street and said to move on. A confrontation with the policeman led to a case before a magistrate in Bow Street.

London's leading morning newspaper, the *Daily Telegraph*, gave a full report of Jenkins's day in court:

"Just before the rising of the court, a coloured man entered with a troupe of thirteen little Negro boys whose ages ranged from five to about fourteen years. The man in charge of the boys said he was the Reverend D. J. Jenkins, a Baptist minister of Charlestown, America, and he wished to make an application to the magistrate. On entering the witness box, the appellant stated that he had come to this country to raise funds for an orphanage with which he was connected in Charlestown. He had brought with him his boys, who all played on brass instruments, and his [applicant's] object was to let the boys play their band in the public streets, after which he lectured and collected money for the orphanage. He had been stopped that morning while thus engaged, and told that he was liable to be taken into custody for what he was doing, and he wished to be informed whether this was so. Sir John Bridge told applicant that of course he must not cause an obstruction in the public thorough-fares or the police would interfere. Inspector Sara, who was on duty in the court, pointed out that under an Act of Parliament no child under the age of eleven years was allowed to sing, play or perform for profit in the public streets. Applicant: But could not an exception be made in my case, seeing the object I have in view? Sir John Bridge: Certainly not, the law makes no excep-tions. Applicant then said he was without money, and it appeared he was not allowed to raise any in the way he hoped to do, and asked the magis-trate if he would give him money to take the children back to America. Sir John Bridge said he had no fund which was available for such a purpose, and advised applicant to apply to the American Consulate. Inspector Sara said he would send an officer with the Applicant to the Society for the Prevention of Cruelty to Chil-dren where probably he could obtain assistance, and Sir John Bridge gave a sovereign to appli-

cant for present necessities, for which he appeared very grateful."

The "Police Intelligence" item provoked a long editorial
in the same issue, which said in part: " . . . Mr. Jenkins's
attempts to procure subscriptions for his orphanage by such
drastic measures as he contemplates should, at any rate, be
tried in the first instance within the pretty extensive borders
of his own land. Whether the sacred cause of charity itself is a
sufficient justification for his proceedings is another question.
Much may be done, no doubt, to raise money for an orphanage; but to let loose a brass band of thirteen negro children
upon an urban population suffering with nerves is likely to
create almost as many orphans as it would relieve."

Sarah Dowling continued her narrative:

> The gloom and horror of the court
> hearing passed and things got better. Par-
> son was invited to preach at London's
> Metropolitan Tabernacle at the Elephant
> and Castle, London, where the imminent
> Charles Haddon Spurgeon, one of the
> greatest British preachers of his time, had
> ministered. Spurgeon was one of Parson's
> heroes. Parson stood in the pulpit and

explained the altercation with the London police. About twenty-five women leapt up and solicited a collection from the church people. Emotion was undisciplined. When the ushers carried the plates back to the altar, they were overflowing with enough English money to take the Americans back home and pay for repairs to the orphanage. But they did not return home then. Other churches invited them to give programs for which they were paid.

Notification came that a 100-acre farm in Annieville, near Ladson and Summerville, had been donated to the orphanage by Deacon Joseph Wild, from Brooklyn, New York. Parson was thunderstruck at finding so many boys suited to work on the farm, whereas none of them would have been considered for the band room.

The bands went north in the summer and south to Jacksonville, Florida, in winter. When bands were not at the orphanage, the children did what they had to do. They had prayer meetings and went to classes.

The orphans worked hard at the pressing club, printing press, and shoe repair shop. The orphanage building was large enough that it could accommodate the trades in the basement. Upstairs is where the orphans lived and went to school. Mrs. Pearline Daniels was one of the best teachers, and she was Parson's church organist. Eloise Harleston came to work as Parson's secretary. She was very smart. The Harlestons were the most prominent black family in Charleston.

The children were not picky like they are today. Parson made every one of them go to church every Sunday morning. When they started to church, they walked up Franklin Street to Beaufain Street, over to Ashley Avenue, and up Ashley to Palmetto, where the church was. It was a long walk.

The children wore clothes that were donated. The clothes were taken to the basement and doled out on a first-come basis. Not all of the boys were able to get clothing suitable for boys. In the rag-tag army of orphans that walked to church on Sunday morning one would see boys wearing high-heeled women's shoes and women's coats, anything they could get. I wish you could have seen the procession, hundreds of orphans on the way to church. When the first ones went into the church, some were still blocks away.

Parson had a child by Eloise. That child, Olive, was born in England, during their tour. Olive was adopted and raised by the midwife who delivered her. Parson was notified to go and get her when she was a teenager. He went to Wigan, England, and brought Olive to New York and kept her there for a week. Parson had opened an office in Harlem, and he wanted Olive to be with people of her color. She had been the second black person ever in Wigan, England.

Later, DuBose Heyward, a man we all knew, wrote *Porgy*, and his wife, Dorothy, wrote the stage play. The man I would marry, John Dowling, was in the play. He traveled to New York and London and said they played to packed houses every night.

After that, the Depression became less severe. People rallied and the band members traveled. There was more than one band on the road at one time. Parson put me to work traveling with the girls chorus. I also filled out applications for incoming orphans and worked at the printing press every Thursday night, printing Parson's little newspaper *The Messenger*. The gossip column "Wide Awake" was the most popular part of the newspaper. It was written by John Dowling and often started like this: "I saw Mr. Ravenel last night" . . . or "Mr. and Mrs. Alston are spending the Christmas holidays at their plantation." . . . After mailing the newspapers, I went home. It usually was 2:00 or 3:00 in the morning.

Lena Jenkins died and Parson married Eloise. Parson was taking in a lot of money, but it was not under his name. Most of it was under the Orphan Aid Society. He gave some to the Harlestons, Eloise's family. Parson actually owned but very little. He had one home that he lived in, at 34 Magazine Street. He owned No. 8 Holmes Street, now called Killins Street.

There came a time when the City Council, who had been giving Parson a stipend for years, questioned him. They believed he was requesting more than he needed. But if he had not taken in those children, they would be out there in the street, with nothing to eat and no place to go. It was like this: a mother would come and say she had a child she could not keep. They came every day. Some mothers left their children on the orphanage steps. I know, because I filled out the admission forms. But running the orphanage took a lot of money.

Securing jobs for orphan girls became a money-making operation for Parson. People from New York who were in need of domestic help called at Parson's Harlem office and asked that any orphanage girl who needed a job come north and work for them. The Clyde Line people gave him a reduced rate. Parson worked out a system whereby he paid for the transportation and sent the girls to New York. The first month's salary was turned over to the Harlem office, where it was sent to Parson as his employment commission and repayment of transportation. So many Jenkins Orphanage girls obtained jobs in New York that the word in Charleston was "Parson Jenkins is a brilliant agent." My dear, that was the beginning of southern black girls going to New York to work for the wealthy people.

My next interview with Mrs. Dowling was at her home on July 26, 1995.

Parson bought forty acres of land on the Ashley River. The tract formerly was Lincoln Park. Incorrigible girls stayed in a building on that property. Bad boys stayed in another building, but if one became too riotous, he was sent to the farm.

Parson owned everything all the way down Bonds to Dorchester Road. He had a little house by the river. Miss Phillips, his secretary, took his notes and typed them. She took down his sermon for the next Sunday. He preached at his church nearly every Sunday in spring, fall, and winter. In the summer he took a three-month vacation and traveled with the band.

Olive and Mildred went to Benedict College together. After Olive got married, she fell on hard luck and Mildred helped her. They were half-sisters and they loved each other. Olive's mother was Eloise, and Lena Jenkins had Mildred about the time of Olive's birth. Now, listen to me: Lena died from a broken heart. She knew about the affair between Parson and Eloise.

On Friday night, March 17, 1933, one hundred and forty-two orphans ranging in age from three to twenty-one were asleep in the orphanage building when someone yelled, "Fire!" Flames were shooting from the roof. An alarm went to the fire station at Queen and Logan Streets.

People were falling all over each other in the darkness, trying to get out. The blind Askew boy, Roosevelt, stood on the second-floor porch. He held out his arms. Tears coursed down his cheeks. A second alarm went in.

A fireman reached Roosevelt, and they started down on a ladder. Roosevelt fell and dangled high above the ground. The fireman pulled him back and they started down again. Roosevelt's body slammed against a burning pillar but the fireman pulled him away. The instant they reached the ground the walls collapsed.

People felt sorry for Parson and donated money. Then a reporter from *Time* Magazine showed up.

The *Time* Magazine article appeared in the Charleston *News and Courier* on August 23, 1935. Reading that story was about the hardest thing Parson ever had to stand up to. Under the heading MUSIC and a photograph of Parson, the story talked about Parson and his "little touring tooters." The piece went on to say that he had become Charleston's Number One citizen, but at 74, he was grizzled, black-garbed, and ailing. And that was the good part. According to *Time*, Parson's bands, numbering 125 players aged ten to eighteen, had toured the United States and Europe, and the musicians worked long hours to earn from $75,000 to $100,000 a year for the Society. They lived at the orphanage, while "rich old Reverend Daniel Joseph Jenkins sat in his plush Harlem offices, scrutinizing detailed weekly reports of his bands' doing."

It was no surprise that Parson took ill. We strained green peas and crackers for his meals. He lounged around and spoke of all the children he had helped with their lives. Most of Parson's own children had tuberculosis and some of them died from it. All of them had talent. They were smart. Stirling was a dentist. His office was on Hasell Street, next to the Catholic Church. Edmund's greatest composition, *Charlestonia*, was presented in the Kursaal of Ostend, the celebrated Belgium summer resort. Mildred traveled all over the world singing. The oldest daughter, Lena, graduated from Howard University. Roxy married Mordecai White, who became a famous musician.

Parson Jenkins died on July 30, 1937, tired and full of days. His wife, Eloise, and his daughters, Mildred and Olive, survived him. At 1:00PM on Tuesday, August 3, 1937, more than 2,000 mourners attended funeral services held at Charleston's Morris Street Baptist Church. Services were held there because the church was larger than the Tabernacle Fourth Baptist Church on Palmetto Street, of which Parson had been pastor for forty-six years. None of the bands that had carried the fame of the Jenkins Orphanage from coast to coast and made trips to Europe were there to play a tribute to the founder of the institution. Seventy band members, playing in three groups, were on the road at the time of Parson's death, playing and singing in Boston, Saratoga, and New York City. Few jazz musicians who had left the orphanage came back to the funeral.

If Parson had lived about ten years longer, he would have doted on the glory that came to his "black lambs" who achieved phenomenal fame. Gus Aitken played with the Louis Armstrong band; Cat Anderson, Freddie Jenkins, Rufus Jones, Leroy Rutledge, and Jabbo Smith went with Duke Ellington; Emmet Perry played with Dizzy Gillespie; Peanuts Holland was with Charlie Barnet; Freddy Bennett played with Luis Russell; Julius Fields achieved fame with Jelly Roll Morton; and on and on.

After Count Basie's death, Freddie Green took over the band. He had delivered the eulogy at Basie's funeral. Many famous musicians could make the statement made by Freddie Green: "I became a jazz musician in a city crowded with them, and it all started with Parson Jenkins."

Closing my eyes now I can still hear the Jenkins band playing "Sweet Sue" and "It's A Sin To Tell A Lie."

Sarah Dowling is in heaven now, I imagine, conversing with her beloved Parson and his "black lambs." During the times we met, she spoke with reverence when she spoke of Parson Jenkins. "Feed my lambs," she said, remembering the end of his sermons. "Feed my black lambs." She could still hear the Charlestonians, when the band played on the streets, calling out "Here comes Jenkins."

Where Are the People?

If I hadn't strolled into the bookstore that day, chances are this story would never have been written.

I noticed a bookstore and ducked inside after finishing my storytelling engagement at a large hotel in Charleston. A sales person came over and asked if she could help me. I told her I was writing a book that included some islands off the coast of Charleston and I planned to interview any people I could find who could tell me stories about an earlier time. I asked if she had any books on islands history or folklore.

Just then a lovely lady walked up to me and said, "Honey, if you're writing a book on the islands, you must include Rockville. It's a village at land's end on Wadmalaw Island, and it remains as it was a hundred and fifty years ago. The big, airy houses built by the planters in order to catch the fresh sea breezes are there, and some old stores are still in existence. Since Rockville was the site of the state's first regattas, the old yacht club is there, almost surrounded by the sea. You must see Rockville from the water, if you can."

The lady's remarks sparked in me a profound curiosity. I

explained to her that it would be impossible for me to view Rockville from the water but I would see it that very day.

I did not catch the woman's name, but it was obvious she was a true Charlestonian. That she knew precisely everything about the subject she discussed I had no doubt. She remains a lady of mystery, a voice of authority, and I would like nothing more than to introduce her to my readers—and to myself—but she was lost in the crowd before I realized the importance of her words.

Back in the car, Sid found Rockville on the map. "It's at land's end," he said, "about a mile or so from the Charleston Tea Plantation." Our plans that day included touring the Tea Plantation. After visiting James and Johns Islands, we drove on to Wadmalaw and were soon at the Tea Plantation. The owners gave us a thorough history of the tea grown there, and we were served iced American Classic and pound cake. I inquired about Rockville and was told that indeed it was one mile away, at land's end.

Rockville was magical. Time seemed to stand still. Huge moss-draped oak trees provided shade from the sun while diamonds, reflected from the sun's rays, danced upon the blue-green water. We saw no people, but it was a neat little village—smart and prim. I made notes on a yellow pad while Sid snapped pictures.

The waterfront houses had green lawns that swept down

Old store fronts, Rockville. Photograph by Sid Rhyne.

to the water. Docks jutted from land's end. A boat was tied to nearly every dock. We found two old storefronts, long out of use, and the yacht club. I remarked to Sid that I had spoken to groups at some swanky yacht clubs but I would trade them all for one invitation to tell my stories at the Rockville yacht club.

We were about to leave the village when out of the corner of my eye I noticed a tiny church in a grove of oak trees. "It's Cinderella's church," I said. "We have to include the small,

gothic meeting house in the book." There were three historical markers in the churchyard, and I carefully made notes of
every word on each marker. The name of the church was Grace
Chapel.

Just before we left, we noticed the cemetery. Whereas everything in the village was well-tended, weeds in the graveyard
were knee-high. We fingered the bricks in the surrounding
wall, and I imagined they came from England as ballast in
sailing vessels. Sid spotted an ancient rusted gate and we entered the cemetery.

An old world lay buried there. Some of the grave markers
were tall with beautiful sculpture. Several served as trellises
for ivy vines. Others lay flat on the ground. We read inscrip-
tions. Some of the deceased had come to the grave full of
years; others had died in their infancy. Sid remarked again
about the weeds and how untidy the cemetery was.

As we drove away, we talked about Rockville being one of
the loveliest places we had visited in our many years in the
South Carolina Low Country. I couldn't get over the fact that
we saw no people.

Back at home, I transferred all of my notes from that day
onto the computer. The very next week we went back to the
islands and proofread my notes for accuracy. We retraced our
steps on James Island and Johns Island, and went on to
Wadmalaw and the Charleston Tea Plantation. Then we en-

tered Rockville. Again, we saw no people in the village.

I read aloud from my computer printout as we walked around. The descriptions of the houses, stores, yacht club, and surroundings were accurate. Then we walked to Grace Chapel before ending our second visit to Rockville. We proof-read my notes against the historical markers. As I followed my notes, we walked toward the ancient cemetery. To our great shock, *there was no cemetery*. Someone had recently mowed a lawn where the cemetery stood a week earlier. Marks from a lawn mower's wheels were evident. You could smell fresh grass cuttings. And this was no new lawn. This lawn had spent years growing.

Let me tell you! To get the full impact of a disappearing cemetery, you *must* view it in a tiny village where you have not seen a single living soul.

Finally I said, "I'd bet on a stack of Bibles this high a cemetery was at this very place last week." When Sid could pull himself together, he said, "Nancy, you've written about so many ghosts they've come back today to haunt you."

"Get in the car," I ordered. "We're going to the Tea Plantation and find out how a cemetery can disappear."

At the Tea Plantation, Sid could barely keep up with me as I made my way up to the office. I confronted the owner, explaining all we had seen.

"There is no cemetery there today, is there, Nancy?"

"No. How can a cemetery disappear?"

"No cemetery is there today because last week Don Johnson and Melanie Griffith were in Rockville making the movie *Paradise*. The cemetery was a movie set."

After that episode, we each needed a big glass of tea!

Needless to say, when the movie came to Myrtle Beach, Sid and I were first in line to see it. We felt special sitting there among the other movie goers, because we had seen the "real" Rockville cemetery.

Several years later when I was deep in research papers at the Caroliniana Library in Columbia, I discovered a document about Rockville. The charming story was written in 1940, when I was in school in North Carolina. The piece was a school project written by Margaret Wilkinson of Charleston. We could have been about the same age. Just as I would never know the woman who came to me in the Charleston bookstore and introduced me to Rockville, it is likely I shall never know Margaret Wilkinson. I trust she received a grade of "perfect" for her work because it is complete beyond improvement in my eyes. It told me everything I wanted to know and never expected to learn about Rockville. My story would not be complete without sharing Margaret Wilkinson's story about Rockville.

Bohicket Creek from the bluff at Rockville on any one of three afternoons the first week of August is the scene of the Low Country's most traditional yacht regatta. Sailing craft of seven classes—from the majestic schooner to the jaunty little snipe—point tall masts against a blue of iridescent sky. They balloon white sails into brisk breezes that pulse in from the Atlantic over the luminous waters of the salt creek.

Rockville, a little village of 300 people, each year under the streamer of the Sea Island Regatta, puts on a "Good Times Show" that will vie with the smartest Broadway review in rhythm, color, romance, beautiful girls. But no New York audience could possibly attain the spirit of sheer fun that sweeps up and down the bluff during Rockville's racing week.

This fun land holds open house. There is no cover charge. Some of the spectators bring picnic lunches and spread them under the trees on the bluff or over a boat deck. Others sit on a roughhewn bench in the country store and stuff down soda pops, cheese crackers, and hot dogs.

All who can possibly do so quarter themselves in the little hamlet. Fresh seafood deliciously prepared and good country fare add to the enjoyment. Debutantes from Charleston or Washington, their friends and chaperones, turn the little schoolhouse into a dormitory and sleep three in a bed or on cots. The lure of the water sports and the spirit of the regatta rather than the dances held every evening at the yacht club pavilion draw these people to Rockville.

Here at least the automobile is not the favorite mode of travel. The boat experiences anew its Cinderella hour when the people of the neighboring sea islands find it jolly as well as convenient to charter a cabbage scow or power launch and head for Bohicket Creek. The old *Mary Draper* and the *Sunbeam* are favorites of the islanders. From over their gunwales come the sound of the tinkle of glasses blended with the strains of "Old

Confeedence" [see page 141] and other images that hark back to the days of the long staple cotton.

Launches bearing private parties patrol the waters. Outboard motor boats steered by sun-tanned youths have pretty girls as figureheads. These rift the waters as they cut between the other boats, criss-crossing narrow deep furrows plowed by the larger craft.

The piers and wharves are spattered with spectators. Bronzed children duck one another or swim in and out among the small boats tied up at the piers.

The sailing committee of the sea island club is as casual as the spectators are informal in spite of the tension among skippers and fans at this season, for the Rockville regatta comes as a climax of the South Carolina racing season. It follows regattas held at Savannah, Beaufort, and Charleston. Rivalry runs high since the following week the crews will haul their craft to Wilmington for the finals of the South Atlantic Racing Association at

Wrightsville Beach.

Yet the Sea Island sailing committee mails no invitations to skippers. To register a skipper need only to sign his name and that of his boat on the bulletin board posted on the town oak which has stood witness to the start and finish of all regattas ever held under the bluff. The course the boats are to follow is also posted here.

Of the larger scow and swallow types there are familiar favorites in Low Country waters. The *Syndicate* has led its class for several seasons. The *Star Dust II*, Wilmington's reproduction of the *Syndicate*, since making her first start in South Carolina waters in 1936 has furnished competition for the *Syndicate* and prevented her from simply walking away with regattas. The *Valkyrie* of Charleston is another of the scow type. The popularity of the *Undine IV* is enhanced by her owner, Mr. Oliver Seabrook, president of the Rockville club. Then there are others, the *Geechee* of Savannah, the *Queen Mary* and the *Carolina* of Wilmington, and *Miss*

Charleston.

At each regatta there is a free-for-all race for the larger boats, and a separate one for the snipes. But almost any race regardless of class may supply the thrill of the afternoon.

When the starting gun fires, a fleet of the sky scraping marconi rigged yachts sweep down Bohicket Creek and head for the Stono River. The other classics follow at five minute intervals. Gradually all the wind-filled sails that cluster together cross the starting line and brush the sky lane seaward above the creek.

The launches trail, carrying a large bulk of the spectators who will see the entire race from start to finish. Those left on the bluff will miss seeing some of the race. They fill in the time with the making of wagers and matching stories. The conversation is as salty as it is doggy among the benches at a Kennel Club Show. An old timer recalls the *Nell*. The *Nell* was built by "Ned" Hall of Mt. Pleasant almost thirty years ago. In her day she outsailed the best yachts on the coast and continued to sail after these had given up and gone. Year after year she was taken to Rockville where she won Sea Island regattas, beating all comers in all breezes until she became a tradition there. Ambitious to beat the *Nell,* Manley Sullivan had two yachts built. Still the *Nell* refused to bow to progress. She remained queen of the local waters, though she did have to bend a bit to the *Bad Penny,* whose skipper used to say, "I never beat the *Nell.* I beat her crew." Then the *Nell* started leaking, became lopsided, and now lies abandoned on the banks of Mt. Pleasant.

While such yarns as this are spun, the *Undine IV* is making yachting history over the course. "It's an *Undine* breeze today," some in the know comment. The phrase passes all along the bluff. The *Undine* gets underway and soon the old champion shows her stern to the fleet. On the first lap out to the sea buoy and back to the starting line there is no threat of anyone's passing her. On the second lap the breeze picks up and the *Valkyrie* gathers speed. Up to the Point of Pines and back again the larger boat cuts down the *Undine's* lead.

The spectators on the barges now in the Edisto River feel the breeze freshening. Smiles wane. The light air holds. As the two boats round the beacon at the mouth of the creek and head into the home stretch, the *Undine* still has a nice lead.

"They'll never catch Olly on the free sheet run," someone is heard to remark. And they do not.

The breeze is so light it seems the Class B boats will not get in until after the judges have gone home to supper. A drifting match takes the place of the race. Then from around the bulbous green summit of the town oak an ominous black cloud raises its head. The breeze becomes a blow. Blobs of rain pimple the smooth waters of the creek.

The *Jacksnipe* heels and turns over out of fear of the big breeze. Two other snipes

do likewise. The big boats get in before the squall strikes. The *Shearwater* and the *Spendrift* finish third and fourth in the only close finish of the day. Coming through the calm the two boats sail fairly evenly, the *Shearwater* gradually stealing away with more wind. She is leading when she rounds the sea buoy but takes a faulty come about and almost stalls. The *Spendrift* is now breezing towards the buoy kicking a furrow. She heels but skims around the buoy gaining on the turn and so goes after the *Shearwater*.

Down the stretch they battle neck and neck. Just as it seems the *Spendrift* is in a position to spurt ahead, she falters and lays on her bottom. Her spinnaker sail is carried away at the foot a few seconds before the two boats are due to cross the finish line, allowing the *Shearwater* a lead of inches. While the big sail is flapping the *Shearwater* creeps a few feet ahead. By the time the *Spendrift* gets her canvas under control again it is too late. The *Shearwater* sits on her edge and plows across the line

exactly ten seconds ahead. It is a photo
finish.

Although Sid and I saw no people at Rockville during
our two visits to the village, it is obvious that thousands have
enjoyed the special beauty of that place.

The lady in the bookstore, whose name I'll never know,
started the adventure. She advised me to see Rockville by water, if I could. I couldn't—and, as it turned out, seeing it by
land did nothing to lessen the magnetism of the place.

"Old Co'feedence"

The best part of each of the tales I tell is the person who told me the story.

Sid and I visited Edisto Island during the 1970s in search of an old-timer who would share stories of bygone days. The country store seemed the perfect place for a storyteller, and the proprietor, Marion Whaley, had an extraordinary gift for remembering details of things past. He seemed to have fallen from heaven, just for me.

Whaley was a groceryman. Islanders and tourists buying produce heard many stories: tales of the ocean, island history, family memories, tales of terror. Each Low Country family has its legends—the Whaleys had more than most. I was especially grateful to meet Marion Whaley because he had lived through the experiences he shared.

The Whaleys were among Edisto's greatest old families. Listening to the groceryman weave his tales, my thoughts traveled back to a choir of old saints rendering Edisto Island's anthem, "Old Co'feedence." This is a memory held by many Edisto islanders.

That day of December 2, 1932, when the Black Strap Minstrel's performance was held on the island was a day for reminiscing. "You remember the eight-oared and ten-oared boats crafted from cypress trees the sea island cotton planters used to transport freight and passengers between the island and Charleston?" someone asked. "Yep. Most of them have gone out of style, but you can see the eight-oars and ten-oars in Charleston, where the fishermen of the Mosquito Fleet use them as fishing vessels when they go for porgo. They sell that fish right smart in Charleston and Kiawah Island."

The most memorable subject brought to issue was the song "Old Co'feedence." It has been as important to an islander as his oar and his rifle. And it was that old rowing song that the Black Strap Minstrel audience longed to hear. The official name of the song was "Old Constitution," composed at Jack Daw Plantation on Frampton's Inlet Creek.

Charlie Bailey owned a plantation at Point of Pines—which Whaley called "Pint o' Pines." Some of his enslaved Africans sang the song as they stood on the bank watching *Old Constitution* come around the bend. The arrival of that boat was a big event for Charlie Bailey's slaves, who were called "Charlie Bailey's chillun." A crowd always gathered on the bank to await the docking of the boat. Some waved palm fronds. The spectators watched in anticipation as the oarsmen, with their enormous muscular arms and massive chests, moved in rhythm, bringing the boat to dock.

The Dodge/Seabrook Plantation, Edisto Island. From the Collections of the SC Historical Society.

Some present at the event tried to recall words to the song the oarsmen sang
as they rowed. Then a woman noticed a
young girl in the crowd who was noted
for her extraordinary soprano voice. Miss
Wilkinson, an Edisto Island school girl,
was called up to the temporary stage to
lead them in song.

Onlookers immediately requested the
old sea chantey that helped propel the
oarsmen through the water to and from
Charleston. The song had been sung in
the girl's ears by Maum Jane Chaplin, who
belonged to Edisto's Murray family. Miss
Wilkinson had heard it since she was a
baby.

Illustrating her song with appropriate
gestures, she raised the gentle voice the
Almighty had given her and cried out for
the sight of *Old Co'feedence*. That aching
melody rings in my ears like the rolling
and crashing of the sea waves round this
island.

Charlie Bailey chillun der watch 'um
Mausa, da boat a-comin'
Charlie Bailey chillun der watch 'um
Co'feedence, Old Co'feedence
Roll in, *Old Co'feedence*

The crowd moved their arms in unison during Miss Wilkinson's song, as if pulling oars through water. It is believed this was the first time the chantey was performed on any sort of stage.

After her performance, Miss Wilkinson spoke about the song. According to Maum Jane Chaplin, she said, the "Lizard and Hoecake" song was usually added to the "Old Co'feedence" chantey. The young girl sang the song again, adding the "Lizard and Hoecake" song as a chorus.

Snake bake a hoe cake
Sat the frog to mind 'um
But frog was good for nuttin'
Till he let the lizard take 'um
Bring back my hoecake
You long tail Venus

The oarsmen sang "Old Co'feedence" at the beginning and end of a voyage, but they were never heard to sing if they were racing a boat. Boats were valuable property. Plantation oarsmen took pride in their job, whether they were racing a boat or hauling produce to and from Charleston.

Sampson Williams, of Edisto Island, remembered:

> Before the war, I row the stroke oar
> on the plantation boat. Ain't a man on
> Edisto could beat me. I leave Seabrook
> place at dayclean. At mid-day I be a-settin'
> in my sister's house in Chas'n. But
> Sampson been Sampson in dem day and
> time.

Marion Whaley and many other old island storytellers are no longer around to weave their tales. But their legends live on.

Here Comes Captain Jussely And The *Hildegarde*

═══════════

Many times when the fog was severe, the *Hildegarde* would be the only boat moving in the Charleston harbor. Daddy judged his course by the ship's steam whistle sounding off Fort Sumter and Castle Pinckney. On extremely foggy days, quite frequently, those on the Charleston docking wharf would kid Daddy—who had a wonderful sense of humor himself—saying they would all run off the wharf with the cry "Here comes Capt. Jussely and the *Hildegarde*." However he always made a perfect landing.

Nancy Jussely Lyle
Rock Hill, South Carolina

When Mrs. Dave Lyle stopped by the table where I was signing books in Rock Hill and introduced herself, her name rang a bell. I told her we had taken a room in a motel on the Dave Lyle Boulevard. She explained that the highway was named for her late husband, who had been mayor of Rock Hill for fourteen years. We have traveled that highway many times since that day, and every time I think of Nancy Lyle.

I also think of Capt. J. E. Jussely, one of the most prominent sea captains of the South Carolina Low Country and Nancy's father. I was blessed when Nancy came into the store that day and began the story that would take years of friendship to complete.

Many coastal children spend their lives at the water's edge watching boats go by. In her youth, Nancy Jussely traveled the waters of the Atlantic from Savannah to Charleston and back again with her sea captain father. She lived the tales of which her friends dreamed.

Nancy and I had spent some time talking about her childhood and her father's life as sea captain when she brought out a heroic scrapbook she and her family put together recounting her father's career. The book began with the birth of John Edward Jussely on June 20, 1878. One account covered his young days at The Ridge, the perfect place for a youngster who loved the sea.

Daddy was born in Duplin County, North Carolina, on June 20, 1878, but he grew up at The Ridge, three miles north of Darien, Georgia. The Ridge was a place of lovely old Victorian homes built by local bar pilots and timber barons during Darien's heyday as a timber-exporting port. Some homes in this quaint village were decorated with gingerbread trim. Almost every house had delicate filigree ornamentation. Daddy spent time on rowboats and small sailboats, fishing, crabbing, clamming, shrimping.

The desire of Jussely's heart was to become a sea captain. Sea captains were gentlemen. They were civilized to each other and to everyone else. To get his license, the state required he apprentice two years on a sailing vessel, legally bound through indenture to a master pilot in order to learn the trade.

In 1900, Jussely sailed on what was to be an eighteen-month voyage. He was an ordinary seaman on the Norwegian full rigged sailing vessel *Norig*, bound from Sapelo, Georgia, to Liverpool, England. He listened carefully as others spoke of their adventures on the oceans of the world, of legendary sea captains, and time spent far away from home on sailing ships.

On the *Norig*, Jussely's jobs included shinnying up the topmost sail on the forward mast, furling the sail as he held on by an arm and a leg, hoping he could secure it before a blast of wind billowed it out and away from him.

When the ship arrived in Liverpool, the customs office seized all except one of Jussely's pipes and packs of tobacco. In spite of that, he made friends with the customs officials. When he ran out of tobacco he hoisted a flag with a knot tied in it. A customs employee would bring him another pack. On the day the ship sailed away, Jussely was in his hammock, running a fever with pneumonia. The only medicines were gin and quinine. He recovered from pneumonia and longed to see his family and friends at The Ridge. It would be a long time, however, before the young sailor was home from the sea.

The ship put in at Cardiff, Wales, and took on a load of coal bound for Buenos Aires. Back at sea, the bullock block on the foresail broke and in the calamity, a sailor broke his wrist. During the emergency everyone seemed eager to give advice, but no one could determine how to set the bone. Passengers and sailors voiced a variety of ill-bred and preposterous conjectures about the matter. When the captain reached a decision, Jussely learned a good lesson about a sea captain's conduct. With poise and tact, the captain stiffened his back and announced the determined solution. Explaining there was no way to set the wrist, he called for the sharpest knife on board and a vat of hot tar. The hand was cut off and the stump dipped in the hot tar. The sail maker sewed the skin over the wound.

When the ship reached Buenos Aires, the crew was allowed ship's leave. Jussely and his buddies noticed the gauchos, cowboys from the vast grassy plains of Argentina. Costumed in colorful trousers with wide silver belts, their necks donned in bright scarves blowing in the wind, the gauchos spent most of their time on horseback. For the first time in his life, Jussely felt an attraction to a way of life off the water. For two days, he and a friend failed to return to the ship. Hunger finally drove them back. the captain put them on bread and water.

The *Norig* took on ballast of rock and sand to make it draw sixteen feet and they sailed around Cape Horn toward Australia, where they took on a load of wheat. From there they went to New Zealand for a load of apples, which were loaded on top of the wheat. They crossed the ocean in thirty-six days and docked at Sapelo, Georgia. The *Norig* had traveled for two years.

Jussely, proficient in reading the compass and plotting a ship's course, was fascinated with navigation. When he took the examination for his Master's License, a three-day test in

Savannah, Georgia, he finished in one day and made a perfect score. He spent the next two years on one of his father's pilot boats, working out of Darien, but the sea pulled at him. His next job was on a tug out of Savannah, sometimes traveling as far away as Puerto Rico. Little did he know then that before his life was over, he would pass the tests that would earn him his Merchant Marine master's license twelve times.

A Savannah newspaper reported on March 18, 1908, that J. E. Jussely of the tug *Forest City* saved the day by scaling the dome and shinnying up the flagstaff and putting a new halyard through the block. Otherwise, there would have been no American and Irish flags rippling in the breeze over the buildings when the St. Patrick's Day parade passed by. Nancy Lyle spoke of what happened next.

> By 1908, Daddy had met Miss Clara Virginia Hinson, director of the public kindergarten in Savannah. She wrote her mother, in Kenansville, North Carolina, about her love for "Capt. Jack" Jussely. "He is a graduate of the Steamship Course. . . . You would gladly put me in his keeping. His devotion and love are strong and he is as true as true can be." An engagement ring arrived from Tiffany's in New York,

and Daddy took his beloved to Thunder-
bolt, a small town that occupies both
banks of the Wilmington River east of Savannah. There he slipped the ring on her
finger. They were married in North Carolina in 1909. In the years to come, they
had three daughters.

Daddy spent two years hauling cargo
for the Navy up and down the coast. He
entered as executive officer and left as captain. After the war, he continued his career in the Navy for nearly seven years.
Then Mama took matters into her hands.

Mama bought Daddy the *Hildegarde*.
He told his friends she wanted to keep
him at home. The vessel was built in
Rhode Island in 1898. It was of wood. She
registered in length 90.0 feet, breath 19.0
feet, depth 6.2 feet, gross tonnage 149.65.
Daddy was master and W. H. Mintz was
engineer.

We children wanted to travel with
Daddy, and Mama arranged for one of us
to accompany him on the *Hildegarde's* voy-
ages between Charleston and Savannah.

The Hildegarde. Courtesy of Nancy Jussely Lyle.

I always was completely at home aboard the *Hildegarde*. Snuggled in the top bunk of the forward stateroom, I listened to the creaking of the ropes and pulleys, and finally was lulled to sleep by the lapping of the water against the ship's sides. Early in the morning, the aroma of fresh coffee, frying bacon, and light, fluffy pancakes drifted up from the galley. I stood on the forward deck during the hustle and bustle of getting underway, with the salt spray from the sea on my face.

The ship plowed through the water with a terrific churning of the propellers. Sometimes I ventured to the engine room, which fascinated me. While on deck, watching the sea grass flatten from the push of the water through narrow chan-nels, or rounding an abrupt curve that caused the waterfowl to take to the air with loud screams of protest, I daydreamed, day-in, day-out.

Leaving Savannah for Charleston, I waved good-bye to Felix De Weldon's fa-mous "Savannah's Waving Girl" sculpture on River Street, and we made the ports of call for the *Hildegarde*.

Our voyage included Haig's Point on Daufuskie Island; Spanish Wells near Hilton Head Island; Jenkins Island; Seabrook Island; Fort Freemont on Saint Helena Island dating from the Spanish-American War, 1898; Parris Island near Beaufort; the Beaufort port of entry; Fenwick Island; Martin Point; and Charleston. The route from Savannah to

Charleston was about 150 miles through the beautiful maze of sea islands. Sometimes the banks were lined with moss-draped oaks and lofty pines, and then the waterway would narrow so that I almost could grasp the rushes and reeds as the *Hildegarde* glided by. I'll never forget my father straining at the wheel to navigate the huge ship. After docking in Charleston, he quickly accompanied me to Onslow's Candy Shop on King Street, to select the candy Daddy always took home to his children. It was great fun for me, but Daddy put in long hours and hard work, and his responsibility was unceasing. He had some leisure. He was a dedicated and loving father and husband. Let me show you a sample of Daddy's logs on the *Hildegarde*.

Saturday, Jan. 27, 1923: This day came in with the wind S., lying alongside of Str. St. John. Cleaning and repairing. No running this day. It is a beautiful day.

<u>Monday, Feb. 5, 1923</u>: This day came in thick. Blowing a gale from NE. Left Martin's Point at 6:00 AM. Arrived at Charleston at 9:30 AM. Went to Carolina Baltimore Dock and discharged 600 sacks sugar. Went to our berth and loaded freight. Hired cook Albert Earnest. Left at 12:40 PM. Arrived at Martin Point at 3:40 PM. All OK. Discharged guano and loaded cabbage. Left at 5:10 PM. Anchored in Mosquito Reach at 8:10 PM. Dark as Hell. Believe me.

<u>Monday, 12 Feb. 1923</u>: This day came in cloudy, wind NE. Left dock at 8:10 AM. Went over for oil. Got there at 8:15 AM. Finished getting oil at 8:40 AM. Left for Charleston at 8:45 AM by way of Beaufort. Arrived at Beaufort at 1:30 PM. OK. Left at 2:08 PM. Arrived at Martin Point 7:40 PM. All OK. So ends this day dark as the Hinges of Hell.

<u>Sunday, Feb. 18, 1923</u>: This day came in clear. Cold wind N lying in Charleston. No work done. Sabbath observed. So ends this day.

<u>Saturday, Feb. 24, 1923</u>: This day came in clear and cold. Lying alongside the Str. St. John. Getting ready for excursion this PM. Left with Editor's Excursion party at 2:00 PM. Arrived back to dock at 5:20 PM. All OK. So ends this day.

<u>Wednesday, March 7, 1923</u>: This day came in clear and cold. Wind W blowing a gale. Left Savannah at 7:00 PM for Sugar Refinery. Arrived at 7:30 AM. Loaded 600 sks of sugar. Went to Gulf Refinery and got oil and arrived back at our dock at 10:45 AM. Left for Charleston by way of Beaufort at 11:30 AM. Arrived Beaufort at 4:30 PM. OK. Discharged freight and tied up for the night. So ends this day clear and cold.

<u>Wednesday, March 21, 1923</u>: This day came in with the wind NE. Lying at dock in Beaufort. Left at 6:00 AM for Savannah. Arrived at 11:00 AM. Broke down. Big Boy came to work at 12:00 M.

<u>Thursday, March 22, 1923</u>: This day came in with the wind S. Lying along side of Str. St. Johns.

Hauled over to Wilkerson Machine Shop at 8:15 AM so machinist could work on engine. Crew working painting boat.

Thursday, May 10, 1923: This day came in with the wind NW. Left Beaufort at 5:00 AM for Charleston. Arrived at Martin Point at 11:20 AM. Left at 12:25 PM. Arrived at Charleston and docked at the Baltimore Carolina docks and discharged sugar. Left at 5:00 PM. Went to the accommodation dock and started unloading and loading. Finished at 11:15 PM. OK. One bad dock to handle freight.

Wednesday, Jan. 23, 1924: Wind West light. Lying at the Edisto dock receiving freight and passengers. Left at 8:15 AM for Charleston. Stopped at Martin Point. Stopped at James Island dock and left bateaux. *Hildegarde* arrived in Charleston at 12:20 PM. Landed at head of accommodation dock. Put off hogs and passengers. Went over to the Clyde Line and put off sweet potatoes for New York. Then went up to the Standard Oil Co. dock and got oil. Came back and tied up. Had fire and boat drill this day.

About that time, fishing trips and harbor excursions began to take over the dwindling freight and passenger service. The Charleston *Sunday News*, May 10, 1925, reported that the *Hildegarde*, under Daddy's command, had taken up her regular summer work of boat excursions. Daddy, assisted by his engineer, Mr. W. T. Mintz, kept up a perfect schedule during the last winter on the Charleston-Sullivans Island run.

During this period, the boat did not miss a single trip on account of fog or bad weather. You might like to see some of Daddy's logs on the Charleston excursions.

<u>Friday, July 4, 1924</u>: Lying at accommodation dock. Left 9:00 AM on fishing trip to Jettys. Got back at 1:00 PM. Carried a small picnic party to Lincoln Park and two excursions around the harbor. Finished up at 12:00 midnight. So ends this day. 1400 passengers.

<u>Tuesday, July 15, 1924</u>: Lying at accommodation dock. 8:15 PM to 11:15 PM out with the First Presbyterian Church excursion. 590 passengers. Everything OK. So ends this day.

<u>Thursday, July 17, 1924</u>: Wind light S and clear. Left 7:30 AM for dry dock. Arrived and hauled out at 9:00 AM. Boat pretty worm eaten in spots. Work done scraping bottom, caulking, carpenters putting in planking. So ends the day. Light winds from the SW and hot.

Captain and Mrs. John Edward Jussely. Courtesy of Nancy Jussely Lyle.

On a trip to Beaufort, during the time of an unusually low tide, the *Hildegarde* ran aground. Her keel broke and before help could arrive the tide arose and water damage to the boat and engine were beyond repair. Nothing was saved, not even the piano. Daddy moved his family to James Island, living on Wando Plantation, close to several relatives. We left James Island and lived for a while on Sullivans Island. Before his retirement, Daddy spent several summers as captain of a deep sea fishing vessel at Myrtle Beach, South Carolina.

Mama had been exposed to a lot of beauty, history, and ornamentation in her gracious family home in Kenansville, North Carolina. She returned to that lovely dwelling, so much in character with the South, for her wedding and the birth of each of her children. It wasn't surprising, then, that somewhat in the manner that she bought the extraordinary vessel the *Hildegarde*, she purchased a home on the water in Mt. Pleasant as a sort of extended anchor to her North Carolina family home.

We all immediately fell in love with the house. Windows and porches overlooked Fort Sumter and the Charleston Harbor, and, being on the water, the interior of the building captured an amazing quality of light. We named it "Harbor View." The spacious Mt. Pleasant home would be our family's dwelling for the next forty years. Mama was an expert pianist. When evening came and she desired to calm down the children, she softly played the *Moonlight Sonata, Because, Libestraum,* and *Fifth Nocturne,* to name a few. During thunderstorms, she played the piano with the pedal to the floor. It worked.

Daddy's many years at sea had made him an early riser. When at home, he always cooked breakfast and took Mama's cup of hot coffee to her bedside, before roaring awake his three sleepyheaded daughters with, "Wake-up, Jacob, day's a-breaking, peas in the pot and hoe-cakes a-baking." Response would be much groan-

"Harbor View," Mt. Pleasant home. Courtesy of Nancy Jussely Lyle.

ing and tucking of heads under pillows. Before long we would get our second wake-up call from Mama, with a gentle, "The time has come for me to rise and wipe the slumber from my eyes, to hail the East and greet the West, and say to God I'll do my best."

Though Nancy Lyle now lives in the South Carolina Upstate, her heart is in the Low Country. Low Country folks do not live only in Myrtle Beach, Georgetown, Charleston, Beaufort, and Savannah. True Low Country folk are everywhere.

GLOSSARY

accommodate	to supply
addendum	a supplement added to a book or story
administrator	one who manages something
allotment	the number of hunted prey allowed each hunter
Almighty	God
altercation	angry dispute
amenities	pleasant qualities
ancient	a time long past
anthem	a hymn, song of praise
Apocrypha	a group of Old Testament books not considered canonical
appellant	one who appeals a case of law
apprentice	a person who works for another to learn a trade
articulate	well-spoken; able to express ideas clearly
ballast	cargo carried for stability
beacon	a guiding signal
bluff	a hill with a steep face
boiling	intensely angry; bubbling
bots	infection caused by the larva of a hotfly
buckra	white people
bulbous	bulging
bulkhead	seawall
buoy	a marked float
cabinet maker	a person who makes furniture
canonical	conforming to ecclesiastical rule
catastrophe	calamity; misfortune
ceramic	made from fired clay
chantey	a sailors' song
chaperone	someone who accompanies a younger person
chivalrous	acting with courtesy, loyalty, and courage
chowder	a soup
churning	stirring; agitating
conjecture	an opinion without sufficient evidence
consulate	the premises of a foreign service officer

crepe sole	shoe sole of rubber pressed into crinkled sheets
debutante	a girl making her debut into society
deterrent	serving to restrain from action
disposed	having a certain inclination
Don Quixote	*Don Quixote de la Mancha*; the lofty and chivalrous hero of Cervante's novel
dormitory	a residence hall
dayclean	dawn
ebb	tide water going toward the sea
ecclesiastical	pertaining to the church
effervescence	bubbling; lively
emporium	a center of trade
extraordinary	beyond what is usual
figurehead	carved figure at a vessel's prow
filigree	ornamental work
frond	a large, finely divided leaf
furrow	a narrow groove
gesture	a movement expressive of an idea
gospel	glad tidings concerning salvation
gunwale	upper edge of the side of a vessel
halyard	line and tackle for hoisting a sail
hamlet	a village
handiwork	work done by hand
happenstance	a thing that happens by chance
heroic	characteristic of a hero
heyday	period of great vigor and enthusiasm
hoist	to raise or lift
hotspots	highly successful and interesting places
hue	a shade of color
humble	modest; plain
immense	vast; very great
impact	the force of one body striking against another
indenture	contract by which a person is bound
inscription	an informal dedication
interpreter	a guide
iridescent	lustrous; changing colors

irreverent	lacking respect
jaunty	smartly effective in manner and bearing
knickers	britches gathered at the knees
liable	legally responsible
loot	a pirate's treasure
lopsided	inclining to one side
luminary	a body that gives light; a celestial body
luminous	radiating light
maritime	coastal; near the ocean
mayor	the chief executive of a town
mode	manner of acting
muse	meditate
nomination	denomination; religious group
ominous	portending evil or harm
overwash	to flood
pastime	a pleasant way to spend time
pavilion	an open shelter
perpendicular	vertical, upright
picky	finicky; fussy
pier	a dock jutting into the water
porcelain	a hard white, usually translucent, ceramic
porgo	a salt water fish
pretext	something intended to conceal the truth
pulpit	church platform from which the clergyman preaches
pulse	a throbbing sensation
pumphouse	building where a water pump is located
rag-tag	a diverse crowd; a mob
recipient	one who received something
regatta	a boat race
reminiscing	remembering
rendezvous	a prearranged meeting
review	a reexamination of a performance
rift	to break wind
right smart	a large amount
riotous	disturbing
schooner	sailing vessel with main and fore masts

scow	flat-bottomed vessel with sloping ends
semblance	a resemblance
sermonical	like a sermon
sheer	transparent; thin
sideboard	a piece of dining room furniture that holds dishes
silhouette	solid black profile or outline of an object
skein	length of yarn wound on a reel
snipe	long-billed bird
soprano	the highest female singing voice
sovereign	a monarch, supreme ruler
sparingly	economically; meagerly
spectrum	an array of particles
spinnaker	a large, triangular sail
squall	a sudden, violent storm or wind
steeped	saturated; soaked
stipend	regular salary
stroke	rub gently
swallow type	deeply forked
triangular	three-cornered
trophy	a prize awarded for an accomplishment
unkempt	dowdy; not well-kept
up-and-down	conversation
vigil	watchfulness
village	a rural hamlet, smaller than a town
wad	a handful of money
wane	to decrease periodically
yacht	vessel for private cruising

About the Author:

NANCY RHYNE is a respected and well-sought-after storyteller and speaker, who has a deep interest in preserving folklore of the Low Country. Nancy lives in Myrtle Beach with her husband Sid, where she continues to research and write.

Other books by Nancy Rhyne include

Alice Flagg: The Ghost of the Hermitage

Carolina Seashells

Chronicles of the South Carolina Sea Islands

Coastal Ghosts

The Jack-O'-Lantern Ghost

John Henry Rutledge: The Ghost of Hampton Plantation

More Tales of the South Carolina Low Country

Murder in the Carolinas

Once Upon a Time on a Plantation

Plantation Tales

Slave Ghost Stories

The South Carolina Lizard Man

Southern Recipes and Legends

Tales of the South Carolina Low Country

Touring Coastal Georgia Backroads

Touring Coastal South Carolina Backroads

Voices of Carolina Slave Children